CAMBRIDGE Global English

for Cambridge Primary English as a Second Language

Learner's Book 4

Jane Boylan & Claire Medwell

Series Editor: Kathryn Harper

Contents

Page	Unit	Vocabulary	Reading/Listening	Speaking/Pronunciation
11–26	1 Our community	Adjectives Families, sports and hobbies Jobs	Read about an inspirational sports player Reading for gist Listen to school helpers talk about their jobs Read and listen to an extract from *The Treasure*	Talk about why families are special School helpers describe their jobs Interview and find out about school helpers Connected speech
27–42	2 Earth and beyond	Adjectives to describe landscapes The solar system Scientific words Natural events	Listen for specific information Read about the planets and orbits Listen to descriptions of natural events Read and listen to a poem called *Not a planet anymore*	Talk about people Contractions Rhyming words
43–58	3 Homes	Rooms in a house Types of houses Adjectives	Listen to children describe their homes Read about an eco-house Listen to children talk about strange buildings Read an extract from *The Hobbit*	Talk about where you'd like to live Intonation in *yes/no* questions
59–60	Check your progress 1			
61–76	4 Food	Food Adjectives to describe food	Listen to children talking about breakfast Read about how chocolate is made Using pictures Read and listen to a poem Read and listen to a story called *Charlie and the Chocolate Factory*	Talk about what you eat for breakfast Linking words Weak forms Rhyming words
77–92	5 Adventures	Different parts of books Describe people Words connect to drawing	Listen to story descriptions Read about how to create a superhero Read for gist Read and listen to an extract from *The Seekers*	Draw and talk about your own superhero Tell a story Read with expressions
93–108	6 Going places	Road safety Travel Descriptive adjectives Verbs of movement	Listen to how children get to school Read about a journey to school in Colombia Read about road safety Listen to a conversation in a tourist office Read and listen to an extract from *Lost in the Desert*	Give directions -ed endings

Contents

Writing/Projects	Use of English	Cross-curricular links	21st-century skills
Guided writing: Write and design a leaflet Write an article about a school helper Write about an inspirational person	Imperatives *both* and *too* Adverbs of frequency Verb + infinitive/*–ing*	**P.E.:** An inspirational sports player	Venn diagrams Comparing and contrasting lives of children **Critical thinking:** Identify positive characteristics in others **Values:** Helping people in our community
Guided writing: Write a fact file Create your own adjective poem Design your space shuttle	Comparatives Superlatives	**Science:** Planets and orbits	Identifying planets in solar system Understanding a description in poetic form **Critical thinking:** Solve a quiz on planets and orbits **Values:** Including people around us
Guided writing: Write about a famous landmark Paragraphs Create a dream home Describe an interesting building	Infinitive of purpose *Yes* / *no* questions *made of* / *made from* Modals of possibility	**Ecology:** The eco-house **Geography:** Peru, famous landmarks in many countries	**Critical thinking:** Talk about buildings and what they might be used for Identifying how we can save energy **Values:** Making visitors welcome
Guided writing: Write a poem Create a tasty treat Find out about where food comes from	*some* and *any* Present passive Quantifiers Connectives	**Geography:** Where chocolate is made	Identifying where food comes from **Critical thinking:** Make links between different types of food and food plants **Values:** Overcoming fears
Guided writing: Write a story Punctuation in dialogues Create your own comic strip Write the ending to *The Seekers* story	Instructions Past simple regular/irregular verbs	**Art and design:** Drawing	Forming opinions about stories **Critical thinking:** Identify key elements of adventure stories **Values:** Being brave
Guided writing: Write a description of a special journey Use *like* as a preposition Design your own safety poster Plan a visit to your town or city	Uses of *get* Giving advice Prepositions of direction Past continuous – interrupted actions	**Health and safety:** Road safety	Understanding road safety issues Designing a town map **Critical thinking:** Compare different ways of getting to school **Values:** Taking advice

3

Contents

Page	Unit	Vocabulary	Reading/Listening	Speaking/Pronunciation
109–110	Check your progress 2			
111–126	7 Australia	Extreme weather Geographical features	Listen to a weather report Read a fact file about Australia Noticing numbers Listen to a presentation about a special animal Read and listen to an extract from *Why the Emu Can't Fly*	Describe the weather in your country Do a presentation about a special animal from your country
127–142	8 Nature Matters	Pollution The environment	Match descriptions to environmental problems Listen to a class survey Read about protecting our planet Comparing and contrasting Read and listen to an extract from *The Future of the Present*	Talk about ways to recycle plastic The contracted form of *will*
143–158	9 School's out	Holiday activities Digital vocabulary Agree/disagree Pack for a trip Respond	Listen to a conversation about a holiday challenge Read adverts for holiday courses Using pictures Listen to two friends talking about a trip Read and listen to a play called *Back to School!*	Talk about a trip Making suggestions Act out a play
159–160	Check your progress 3			

Contents

Writing/Projects	Use of English	Cross-curricular links	21st-century skills
Guided writing: Write a blog post about your weekend Make an endangered species poster Be international weather reporters	Present perfect Present continuous for future meaning	**Geography:** Australia, climate **Maths:** High numbers **Science:** Animals	Comparing countries Understanding traditional stories **Critical thinking:** Sort and classify animals according to their key features **Values:** Not being jealous
Guided writing: A personal recount Facts and opinions Make a poster Design your own recycled monster	Defining relative clauses Will for promises Have to express obligation	**Environment:** Protecting our planet	Understanding what we can do to protect the planet **Critical thinking:** Make personal choices about protecting our planet **Values:** being responsible for our environment
Guided writing: Write an invitation Capital letters A nature trail map Create a short play	Would like for invitations Going to for future plans	**Digital literacy:** Understanding the features of a webpage Internet safety and using appropriate language	Interpreting advertisements **Critical thinking:** Compare information and make choices about holiday challengesl **Values:** Being sympathetic

How to use this book: Learner

How to use this book

In this book you will find lots of different features to help your learning.

What you will learn in the unit or lesson.

> **We are going to...**
> - **talk** about why families are special

Big questions to find out what you know already.

> **Getting started**
> What can we discover on planet Earth and in our solar system?
> a Look at the photo of Earth. What can you see?
> b What can you see around Earth?
> c How do you think this photo was taken?

The key words feature includes vocabulary from other subjects, Academic English terms and instruction words.

> **Key words: P.E.**
> **warm up** prepare your body for exercise.
> **stretch** to extend your body, arms or legs.
> **score** win a point in a competition.

Language detective boxes help you find out more about the main grammar in a unit.

> **Language detective – Defining relative clauses**
> **Who** and **that** give extra information about a person.
> An **environmentalist** is someone **who** looks after our natural world.
> **Which** and **that** give extra information about an object, place or thing.
> **Air pollution** is something **that** is dangerous for our health.

Helps you remember other grammar.

> **Language focus – Imperatives**
> Use imperatives to encourage people to do things.
> **Buy** your ticket now!
> **Come** and **join** us!
> **Enjoy** a day out!

6

How to use this book

At the end of each unit, there is a choice of projects to work on together, using what you have learned. You might do some research or make something.

> **1.6 Project challenge**

Project A: A day in the life of a school helper

Write an article about a school helper. Use the information from your interview in lesson 1.3 to create a school helper display.

1. In a group, design a large map of your school. Include all the places and rooms where the school helpers work.
2. Read the interview you did with a school helper again or listen to it again if you recorded it.
3. Write your article and display the interview.
   - Type up on a computer or write your article neatly.
   - Pin it to the school map you designed, in the room or place they work in.
   - Present in class or school assembly.

Questions to help you think about how you learn.

What did you enjoy about doing your project?

Tips you can use to help you with your learning.

Speaking tip

Fluency: connected speech

What time **do you** start? = What time **d'you** start?

What **do you** do in your job? = What **d'you** do in your job?

This is what you have learned in the unit.

Look what I can do!

Write or show examples in your notebook.

- I can talk about why families are special.
- I can understand an article about an inspirational sports player.
- I can ask questions to find out general information about school helpers and their jobs.
- I can write a leaflet about an event in my community.
- I enjoyed a story about special people in *The Treasure*.
- I can write about a school helper or an inspirational person I know.

Games and activities that cover what you have learned in the previous 3 units. If you can answer these, you are ready to move on to the next unit.

Check your progress 1

1. Read the clues and guess the words.
   a. This person is your mother's father.
   b. This adjective means very, very cold.
   c. This rocket can travel into space and come back again.
   d. This adjective describes a house with lots of space.
   e. This type of house has only one floor and no stairs.
   f. This person cleans and fixes things in your school.
   g. This machine can move across the surfaces of planets and moons.

Audio is available with the Digital Learner's Book, the Teacher's Resource or Digital Classroom

Video is available with Digital Classroom

How to use this book: Teacher

Lesson 1: The **Think about it** session introduces the topic through topic vocabulary activities

Engage with the topic of the unit and generate discussion using the image, the video and the big question.

The opening lesson includes Listening.

In this lesson you'll find Language detective and Key words boxes.

Lesson 2: The **cross-curricular** lesson prepares learners to learn in English across the curriculum.

Grammar is presented through an active learning approach.

A non-fiction text exposes learners to cross-curricular language.

Lesson 3: The **Talk about it** lesson develops learners' speaking skills.

Listening models and speaking tips help provide scaffolding for speaking.

Pronunciation is supported through paired activities.

8

How to use this book

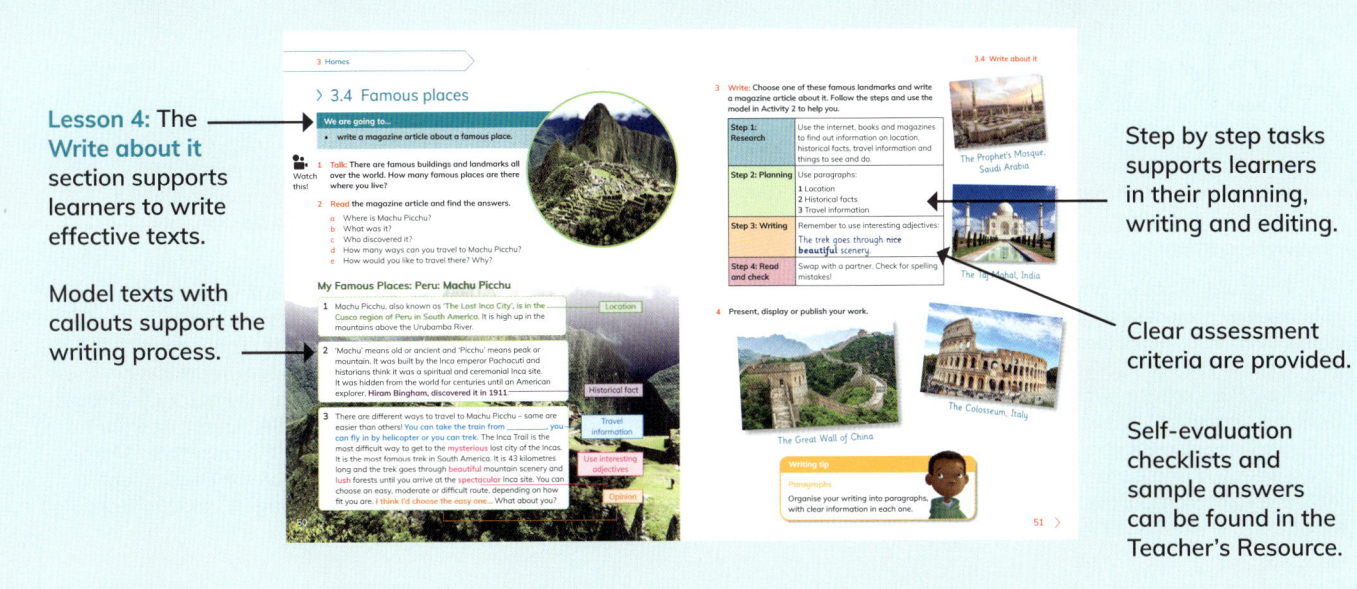

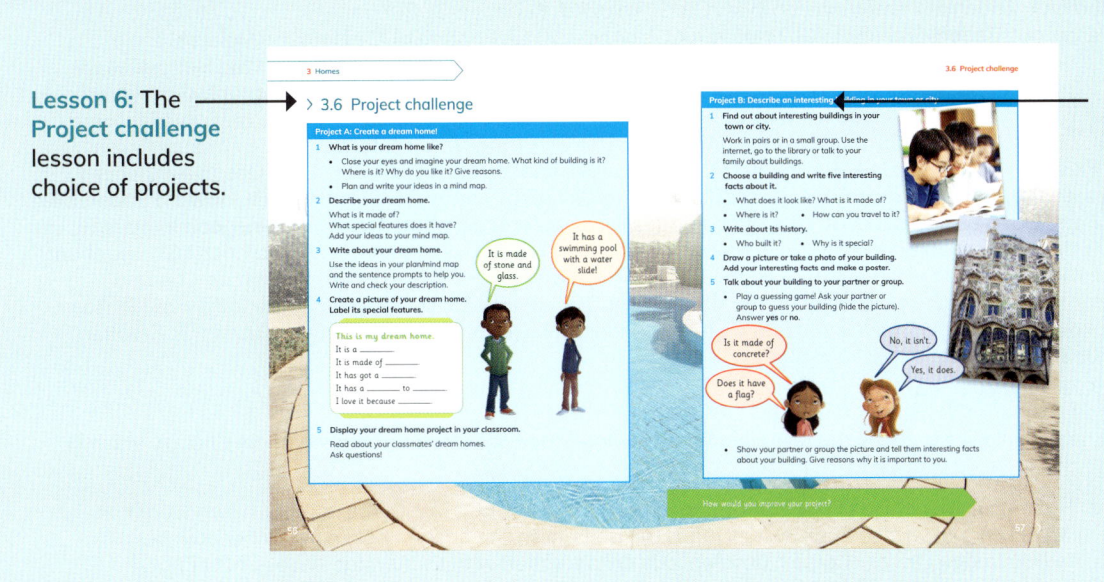

Lesson 4: The **Write about it** section supports learners to write effective texts.

Model texts with callouts support the writing process.

Step by step tasks supports learners in their planning, writing and editing.

Clear assessment criteria are provided.

Self-evaluation checklists and sample answers can be found in the Teacher's Resource.

Lesson 5: The **Read and Respond** session includes literature. This might be a fictional story, a poem or a play.

The audio can be played the first time you meet the story, before learners read the text.

The literature is used as a platform for work on values.

There will be opportunities to think critically about the text.

Lesson 6: The **Project challenge** lesson includes choice of projects.

Projects encourage 21st-century skills such as research, collaboration, and creativity.

Self and peer-evaluation checklists for projects are available in the Teacher's Resource.

9

Acknowledgements

The authors and publishers acknowledge the following sources of copyright material and are grateful for the permissions granted. While every effort has been made, it has not always been possible to identify the sources of all the material used, or to trace all copyright holders. If any omissions are brought to our notice, we will be happy to include the appropriate acknowledgements on reprinting.

'The Treasure' is based on 'The Gift' by Jennifer Holladay, adaptation translation reprinted with permission of Teaching Tolerance, a project of the Southern Poverty Law Center www.tolerance.org; 'Not a Planet Anymore' by Joshua Seigal, reproduced with permission of the author; excerpt from *The Hobbit* by J.R.R. Tolkien, first published 1937, reproduced with the permission of HarperCollins; 'The Seekers' is a summary of part of 'The Seekers' by Valerie Bloom created for *i-read Fiction 4*, edited by Pie Corbett, published by Cambridge University Press, 2006; Extract from *Charlie and the Chocolate Factory*, by Roald Dahl, text copyright © 1964, renewed 1992 by Roald Dahl Nominee Limited. Used by permission of Alfred A. Knopf, an imprint of Random House Children's Books, a division of Penguin Random House LLC. All rights reserved; 'Lost in the Desert' by Margo Fallis, adapted and used with permission; 'Why emus can't fly' is retold from an Aboriginal story; *'The Future of The Present'* by Malini Venkataraman, reproduced with the permission of Jeydevi Venkataraman (Malini is currently studying at Lakshmi School, Madurai, she was in 5th grade when she wrote this story).

Thanks to the following for permission to reproduce images:

Cover illustration by Omar Arandar (Beehive Illustration); *Inside* Chapter 1 Thomas Barwick/GI; Marko Geber/GI; Thomas Barwick/GI; Yellow Dog Productions/GI; Kali9/GI; Monty Rakusen/GI; Caiaimage/GI; Alex Mares-Manton/GI; blue jean images/GI; Maskot/GI; Josh Lefkowitz/GI; Monkeybusinessimages/GI; AndreyPopov/GI; Fertnig/GI; SDI Productions/GI; XiXinXing/GI; Hemera Technologies/GI; Robert Warren/GI; Eric Audreas/GI; Pavel1964/GI; Hill Street Studios/GI; Catherine Falls Commercial/GI; Jupiterimages/GI; Aaron Foster/GI; Kalistratova/GI; Hadynyah/GI; Mevans/GI; SvetlanaSF/GI; JohnnyLye/GI; MB Photography/GI; FrankRamspott/GI; Kativ/GI; Janrysavy/GI; Nerthuz/GI; Nerthuz/GI; Rwarnick/GI; John Sirlin/GI; Neil Irving/GI; Kamil Nureev/GI; Tatiana Gerus/GI; Eerik/GI; da-kuk/GI; HadelProductions/GI; 3DSculptor/GI; Stocktrek Images/GI; VICTOR HABBICK VISIONS/GI; Joe Drivas/GI; Jim Sugar/GI; shunli zhao/GI; Scott Frew/GI; adventtr/GI; lillisphotography/GI; Ewg3D/GI; YinYang/GI; Scanrail/GI; Francesco Vaninetti/GI; MaryAnne Nelson/GI; Adam Crowley/GI; Fitzer/GI; MR1805/GI; thanks to www.simondale.net; Ezra Bailey/GI; UniversalImagesGroup/GI; David Crockett/GI; CJMGrafx/GI; ullstein bild/GI; gsheldon/GI; John Dillon/GI; Pawel Libera/GI; Constanza Halebry/GI; Constanza Halebry/GI; orhandurgut/GI; Somchaisom/GI; AndreyKrav/GI; Axz66/GI; Pictorial Press Ltd/Alamy Stock Photo; 500px Asia/GI; Anna Gorin/GI; PaulVinten/GI; Imtmphoto/GI; CiydemImages/GI; Wolfgang Kaehler/GI; Georgeclerk/GI; Niedring/Drentwett/GI; COSPV/GI; AdrInJunkie/GI; DDurrich/GI; FG Trade/GI; Energyy/GI; Hadynyah/GI; Nick Brundle/GI; Oatpixels/GI; Jill Ferry/GI; Linda Burgess/GI; Hyrma/GI; Hyrma/GI; Boonchuay1970/GI; JohnGollop/GI; EVAfotografie/GI; Tim UR/GI; Floortje/GI; Peter Dazeley/GI; Dimarik/GI; Thomas Imo/GI; Fjmolina/Shutterstock; Science Photo Library/GI; Image Source/GI; Aiselin82/GI; Prani Teiyng Ketu/GI; Taitai6769/GI; Tim UR/GI; Kovaleva_Ka/GI; Tim Hawley/GI; Boonchuay1970/GI; CHARLIE AND THE CHOCOLATE FACTORY, 2005, TIM BURTON, WARNER BROS. (x4) Allstar Picture Library Ltd./Alamy Stock Photo, Album/Alamy Stock Photo, Moviestore Collection Ltd / Alamy Stock Photo, AF Archive/Alamy Stock Photo; TheCrimsonMonkey/GI; TeresaKasprzycka/GI; Flashpop/GI; istetiana/GI; Joe Raedle/GI; Migfoto/GI; Jamie Grill/GI; Radoslav Zilinsky/GI; Yuri_Arcurs/GI; Medesulda/GI; Andresr/GI; Monkeybusiness/GI; Eternity in an Instant/GI; Dulyanut Swdp/GI; Georgeclerk/GI; shaunl/GI; Winhorse/GI; Joeravi/GI; Paul Souders/GI; Westend61/GI; Cassandra Kosmayer/GI; gangliu10/GI; John Borthwick/GI; Mario Marco/GI; Atlantide Phototravel/Corbis/VCG/GI; kolae/GI; Bubaone/GI; Bubaone/GI; Darya Maksimchykava/GI; Doug Byrnes/GI; Westend61/GI; Jeff Greenberg/GI; Photomick/GI; gangliu10/GI; Photomick/GI; Natasha Maiolo/GI; Simonbradfield/GI; Jeff Hunter/GI; Willowpix/GI; Alan Majchrowicz/GI; Matthew Davidson/GI; Jim Reed/GI; Mike Hollingshead/GI; Enrico Ladusch/GI; John Crux Photography/GI; TED MEAD/GI; Tambako the Jaguar/GI; Traceydee Photography/GI; hidesy/GI; Minden Pictures/Alamy Stock Photo; Peter Dazeley/GI; Sean White/GI; Strmko/GI; Michael Brooke/GI; Jamie Lamb/GI; Jami Tarris/GI; askmenow/GI; TED MEAD/GI; Natalyon/GI; YinYang/GI; brians101/GI; Urfinguss/GI; Adam Berry/GI; Lorenzo Quinn and Halcyon Gallery; "Plastic Whale" by Dafne Murillo (2014), mixed media, Image courtesy of Bow Seat Ocean Awareness Programs (https://bowseat.org/); slavadubrovin/GI; Koya79/GI; Xinzheng/GI; LdF/GI; Design56/GI; mixetto/GI; Howard Shooter/GI; Seamind Panadda/GI; Peter Dazeley/GI; peizais/GI; Education Images/GI; ondacaracola photography/GI; Blue Jean Images/GI; Hill Street Studios/GI; SolStock/GI; Adirekjob/Shutterstock/GI; Anthony Devlin/GI; Monkeybusinessimages/GI; Ja'Crispy/GI; piyaphun/GI; Adventure Photo/GI; Anastasiia Shavshyna/GI; Blue Jean Images/GI; njekaterina/GI; Uwe Krejci/GI; Sebastian Condrea/GI; Floortje/GI; die-phalanx/GI; JohnnyGreig/GI; krisanapong detraphiphat/GI; assalve/GI; M.M.Sweet/GI; Elenathewise/GI; Ron Evans/GI; Anastasia Yakovleva/GI; Chad Case/GI; Aluxum/GI; Noel Hendrickson/GI; THEPALMER/GI; Ivan Kuzmin/GI; Stephen Simpson/GI; Westend61/GI; EschCollection/GI; Yagi-Studio/GI.

Key: GI = Getty Images

The authors and publishers would like to thank the following for reviewing Stage 4: Meltem Bottomley, Nidhi Chopra, Vaishali Raheja, Judith Barros.

Development of this publication has made use of the Cambridge English Corpus (CEC). The CEC is a multi-billion word computer database of contemporary spoken and written English. It includes British English, American English and other varieties of English. It also includes the Cambridge Learner Corpus, developed in collaboration with Cambridge Assessment English. Cambridge University Press has built up the CEC to provide evidence about language use that helps to produce better language teaching materials.

1 Our community

We are going to...

- **talk** about why families are special
- **read** about an inspirational sports player
- **use** different verb patterns to talk about what we like
- **write** a leaflet about an event in our community
- **enjoy** a story about special people in *The Treasure*
- **write** about a school helper or an inspirational person we know.

Getting started

What is a community?

a Look at the photos and match the words with the pictures.

school   family   sports team   community helper   neighbourhood

b What is special for you about each of these communities? Complete these sentences. You can choose a word or write your own.

Family is... _loving_.

School is... _____

My team/club is... _____

My street/block is... _____

fun   ~~loving~~   fair   friendly   lively   fantastic   helpful   brilliant   caring

Watch this!

1 Our community

> 1.1 Why are all families special?

We are going to...
- talk about why families are special.

1 **Vocabulary:** Can you name the family members in each photo? What are the differences and similarities between these families and your own?

2 Complete the family word chart. Describe your family to your partner.

| cousin | brother | mum | granddaughter | aunt | sister | ~~dad~~ |
| grandson | grandpa | daughter | uncle | grandma | son |

Male	Female
dad	

I've got an uncle and three aunts.

1.1 Think about it

3 **Listen** and number the photos in activity 1.

4 What's special about each family? Complete the sentences.

sports   animals   new technology   music

a They **love** _____.
b They **are into** _____.
c They **really like** _____.
d They **are keen on** _____.

5 **Talk:** Interview your partner about their family.
Use the expressions in activity 4.
Think of another question of your own.

a How many people are there in your family?
b Have you got any brothers or sisters?
c Where does your family live?
d Have you got any pets?
e What does your family like doing together?
f What's unique about your family?

Language focus

both, too and but

We **both** have two grandmas.
I have a dog **too**.
My cousin has a cat, **but** I haven't.

6 Complete the diagram for you and your partner.

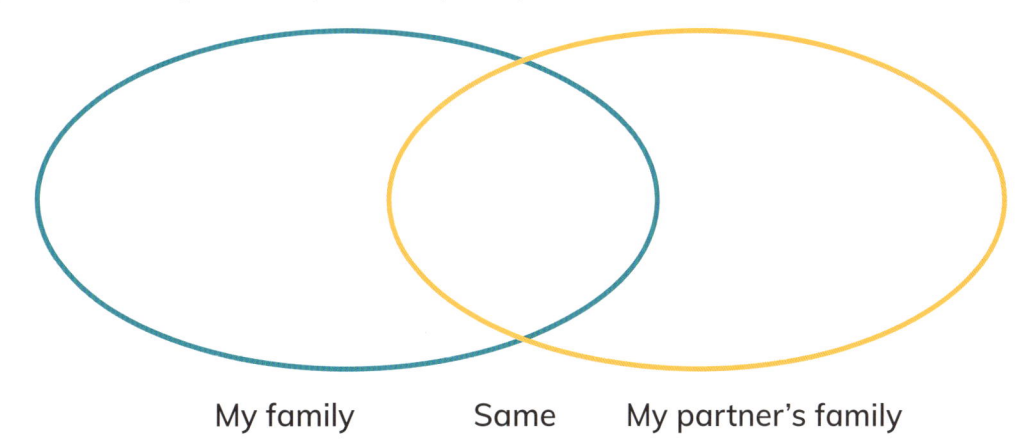

My family   Same   My partner's family

7 Talk about similarities and differences with your partner.
Present to the class.

We both have a cat.

13

1 Our community

> 1.2 An inspirational sports player

We are going to...
- use different verb patterns to talk about what we like
- read about an inspirational sports player.

1 **Talk:** Work in pairs. Do you play any of these sports? Which are your favourite sports? Which sports can you see in the pictures?

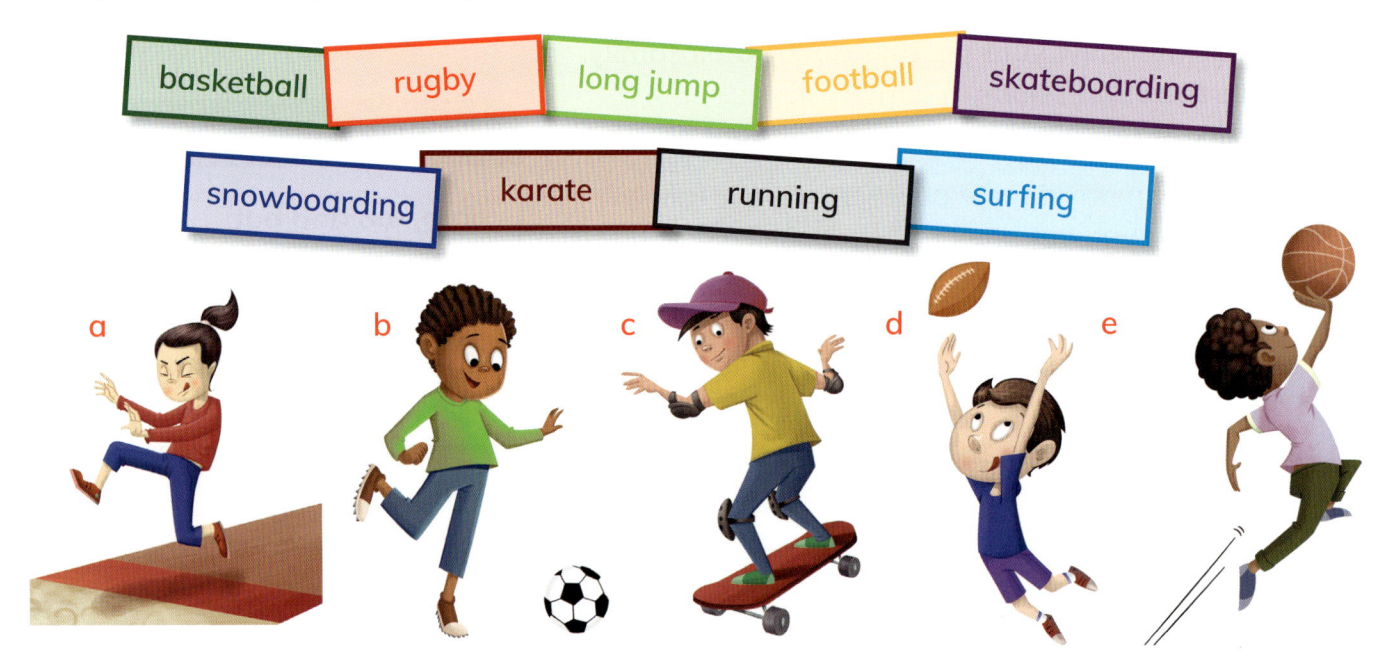

basketball   rugby   long jump   football   skateboarding

snowboarding   karate   running   surfing

a   b   c   d   e

2 **Read** about the sports star Ezra Frech on page 15. Which of the sports in activity 1 doesn't he play?

3 Match the headings with the paragraphs. Listen and check your answers.
   a   School teams and competitions
   b   Ezra's training
   c   Ezra's hopes and dreams
   d   What's special about Ezra?
   e   Family support

4 Play a game. How does Ezra train for basketball?
   Mime the verbs in bold in paragraph 4 to your partner. Take turns.

5 Use of English: Look at the Language detective and write sentences about yourself and your family using the verbs below.

love   hope   enjoy   want   learn

Ezra Frech

1. Ezra is an athlete. He was born without his left knee and got an artificial leg when he was only 11 months old. He has always shown lots of determination and sporting ability. As a baby he even liked throwing and catching balls!

2. He is lucky because he has a loving and caring family. 'My son's incredible,' said Ezra's dad. 'He just gets out there and plays for the team.' He has a motto: 'You can dream it, you can hope for it or you can make it happen!' and that's what he does. He has two younger brothers, who he loves playing sports with too.

3. At school Ezra likes playing all kinds of sport. He's in the school football and basketball teams and he also competes in track and field events such as the 400 metres and long jump. He's competed in championships and has won lots of medals!

4. Ezra does basketball training every day because it makes him feel good. First, **he warms up** by running some laps of the court and then **he stretches** his back and arms. Then he **practises throwing the ball** into the net. He has excellent shooting skills and **scores** lots of baskets in competitions. He **dribbles the ball** and **passes it** to his teammates. Then he **practises his spin moves** before he **cools down** by stretching his muscles again.

5. Ezra learned to skateboard some years ago, which was quite difficult. He also likes surfing and wants to learn to snowboard in the winter. When he's older he hopes to be a champion Paralympic athlete.

> **Language detective**
>
> verb + *ing*
> He enjoys **playing** all kinds of sports.
>
> verb + infinitive
> He **hopes to be** a champion Paralympian.

> **Key words: P.E.**
>
> **warm up** prepare your body for exercise.
> **stretch** to extend your body, arms or legs.
> **score** win a point in a competition.

6. **Talk:** Do you play or like a sport? How do you train for this sport? Tell your partner using verbs in activity 5 to help you.

7. Identify three difficulties Ezra faces in everyday life.

I love playing basketball. I train...

1 Our community

1.3 Our school community

We are going to...
- interview people who make our school a great place to learn!

I do exercise in the sports hall.

1 **Talk:** Look at the list of school places and rooms. What do you do or what do other people do in each place or room?

- Playground
- Library
- Dining hall
- Headteacher's office
- Sports hall
- Classroom
- Music room
- Kitchen
- Cleaning cupboard
- First-aid room

2 **Vocabulary:** Match the jobs to the people.

cook   headteacher   class teacher   caretaker   school nurse   librarian   P.E. teacher

3 How do the adults in school help you? Match the sentences. With a partner, talk about other things they do.

School job
1 teacher
2 cook
3 librarian
4 P.E. teacher
5 caretaker
6 nurse

How do they help me?
a prepares my lunch
b keeps me fit
c cleans and fixes things in my school
d lends me books
e looks after me if I'm ill or hurt
f teaches me lots of new things

1.3 Talk about it

4 **Listen** to the three school helpers talking about their jobs. Who are they?

5 **Listen** again. What's special about their jobs?

Language detective – Adverbs of frequency

never   hardly ever   sometimes   usually   always

0%   50%   100%

I **sometimes** work on Sunday mornings.
I **always** get up early.
I **usually** ride my bike to school.

6 **Talk** about what school workers do for you.

   a   Who always gets up to open the school gates?
   b   Who sometimes works on a Saturday morning?
   c   Who is always in the school kitchen?
   d   Who usually takes 10 minutes to ride to school?
   e   Who works from 9 a.m. to 4 p.m.?
   f   Who usually fixes things in the school?

7 In groups, decide which school worker each classmate is going to interview. Together write the questions you want to ask.

   What's your job?
   What time do you usually start/finish?
   What's special about it?
   What the best/worst part of your job?

8 **Pronunciation:** Listen and repeat the sentences.

Speaking tip

Fluency: connected speech

What time **do you** start? = What time **d'you** start?

What **do you** do in your job? = What **d'you** do in your job?

9 **Talk:** Arrange a time to interview the school worker in your classroom.

   - Ask the questions you have prepared.
   - Write their answers in note form.
   - Record the interview.

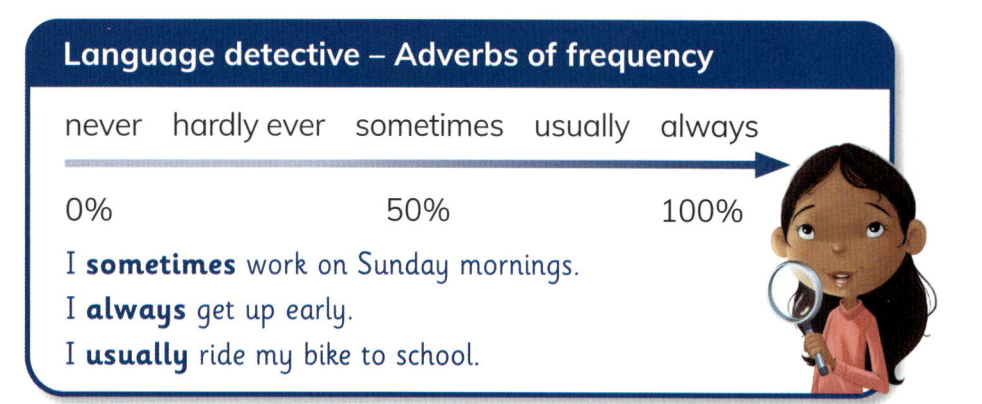

1 Our community

> 1.4 Organise a community event

We are going to...
- write a leaflet about an event in our community.

1 Talk: Look at these leaflets about different events in a community. Which event do you like best and why? Tell your partner.

Family Fun Day

Honeycombe school field
Saturday 5th July from 10–3 pm

- bouncy castle
- face painting
- sculpture painting
- treasure hunt
- live music
- horse rides

Come and join us for a Family Fun Day!
Activity pass: $3.
Help keep Honeycombe school open!

Why don't you come to Spelling Bee Day? Bring all the family! Are you good at spelling?

Where: Community centre
Date: 6th April
Time 5pm

[Date of event]

Charity: We're raising money for the local animal shelter.

3K Family Fun Run!

Location: Abbey Fields

Date and time
3rd May 10 am start.
Arrive at 9.30 to get your number and warm up.

[Time of event]

[Imperatives]

Come and enjoy a great morning with all the family! We're raising money for Royal Children's Hospital!

---

2 Read the leaflets. Are these sentences about the events **true** or **false**?

a	The Family Fun Day is held at the weekend.	true / false
b	There are five different activities you can take part in.	true / false
c	The Spelling Bee event takes place in the local library.	true / false
d	It's to raise money for pets that don't have a home.	true / false
e	The Fun Run is only for adults.	true / false
f	You need to get there 30 minutes before the start of the race.	true / false

1.4 Write about it

3 Write the answer. Which event is for you if...
   a you are into sports? _____
   b you enjoy reading? _____
   c you want to raise money for the local children's hospital? _____
   d you don't have plans on Saturday? _____
   e you are keen on craft activities? _____

> **Language focus – Imperatives**
>
> Use imperatives to encourage people to do things.
> **Buy** your ticket now!
> **Come** and **join** us!
> **Enjoy** a day out!

4 These are slogans. We write them when we want people to come to an event or buy something. Match these slogans to an event in Activity 1.

   Join us at the local community centre!

   Run for Royal Children's Hospital!

   Come and try sculpture painting!

   Buy your activity pass today!

5 **Write** and design a leaflet for the 'Big Clean up'.

Step 1: Research	In groups, decide on: • a local charity you want to raise money for • a place in your town or at school that needs a 'big clean up'. Take photos if possible.
Step 2: Planning	Decide on: • a date and time for the event • what needs doing/cleaning up • how to organise the clean-up (groups) • how to raise the money.
Step 3: Writing	Draw pictures. Find photos. Remember to write a slogan too.
Step 4: Read and check	Swap with a partner. Check for spelling mistakes!

6 Present, display or publish your work.

1 Our community

> 1.5 The Treasure

We are going to…

- enjoy a story about special people in *The Treasure*.

1 **Talk:** In pairs, look at the pictures. What treasures do you think the children find?

2 **Read** and listen to the story *The Treasure*. Check your ideas.

The Treasure

Mrs Damla, the class teacher, gave out the pieces of paper. 'This is your homework for the weekend, children.' The children groaned. It was Friday and
5 they didn't usually get homework over the weekend. 'Your homework is to follow the map of your neighbourhood and to find the treasure at the places marked with an X on the map.'

10 Omer put up his hand. 'Are there really treasures hidden in our neighbourhood, Mrs Damla?'

'Of course there are,' she said.

The final bell rang and everyone ran
15 out of the door. 'Yippee! It's Friday!'

---

3 Answer these questions before you read the next part of the story.
   a   What is the children's homework?
   b   Why aren't the children happy?
   c   Why did the children run out of the door?

1.5 Read and respond

Omer sat in his bedroom looking at the map. He didn't want to do homework at the weekend, but a treasure hunt sounded like good fun.
20 He looked at the first X marked on the map. It read 'Omer's house!' He laughed.

'So I'm the first treasure. That's funny!' He called his mum. 'Do you think I'm a
25 treasure, Mum?'

'Of course I do,' she replied.

There was a knock at Omer's door. It was his friend, Azra.

'What do you want to do?' she asked. 'We could play online or watch a film.'

30 'Why don't we do the treasure hunt today instead?' said Omer. 'We'll find the treasure before everyone else.'

'Good idea,' said Azra. 'Let's go!'

---

4 Are these sentences **true** or **false**?

a	The first X on the map was Omer's house.	**true** / **false**
b	Omer wanted to play online.	**true** / **false**
c	Azra thought it was a good idea to go on the treasure hunt.	**true** / **false**

They went to the park first because there was an X marked on the park on the map. Omer and Azra looked everywhere. They looked on the slide and under the swings. They looked
35 in the sandpit and in the trees too, but they couldn't find any treasure.

'Where is the treasure?' said Omer, shaking his head. It was a hot afternoon. 'Look, there's Mr Polat, the ice-cream man. He's selling his delicious ice-creams! Let's get one. I've got some money.' As always, there was a queue of people, but it was worth the wait.

'That's three dollars please, Omer.'

40 'Oh dear,' said Omer. 'I've only got two. I'm sorry, Mr Polat!'

'Don't worry, take it. It's a very hot day. You can bring me the rest of the money tomorrow.'

'Thank you, Mr Polat, you're so kind.'

1 Our community

The rest of the afternoon the two children spent visiting all the places marked with an X on the map. They went to the library to see the librarian.

45 'Do you have any treasures hidden in your library, Mrs S?'

'Oh, I have lots of treasures, children. This is one of them,' she said, holding up a book. 'Would you like to read it together in the reading corner? There are some homemade cakes on the table too.'

On the way home, they met the local police officer, who helped them cross the road.

50 'Have you seen any hidden treasure?' asked Omer. The police officer shook his head and laughed his big, deep laugh that always made the children laugh. Then they asked the gardener, who was planting some beautiful flowers outside the community centre, and after that the vet, who was carefully carrying two kittens into his surgery. They shook their heads too.

55 The children arrived home with no treasure, but they had really enjoyed looking for it.

1.5 Read and respond

5 Trace Omer and Azra's route on the map.

On Monday at school, Omer was worried. They had found no treasure. Mrs Damla came
60 into the classroom and smiled. She pressed a button on her computer and a definition popped up on the whiteboard. 'Community: all the people
65 living in a particular area or place'. 'Communities are full of treasures, children,' said Mrs Damla. 'Think for a few minutes. What are the real treasures in a community?'

70 Omer thought for a few minutes. He thought about the great afternoon he'd had with Azra: playing in the park, the delicious ice-cream from kind Mr Polat, the great story they read in the library, the police officer's really funny laugh.

The people in my community are the treasures, thought Omer.
The treasures were there all along!

COMMUNITY: all the people living in a particular area or place.

---

6 Word study: Read the story again. Find these words.

   a the names of six community helpers
   b three things you can find in a park
   c baby cat
   d two types of food

7 Values: Helping people in our community

Work with a partner to answer the questions.

   a Why does the author use the word 'treasures' in the story?
   b Are there 'treasures' in your home, school or local community?
   c How do these people help in your community?
   d How could you and your class help in your community?

1 Our community

> 1.6 Project challenge

Project A: A day in the life of a school helper

Write an article about a school helper. Use the information from your interview in lesson 1.3 to create a school helper display.

1. In a group, design a large map of your school.
   Include all the places and rooms where the school helpers work.

2. Read the interview you did with a school helper again or listen to it again if you recorded it.

3. Write your article and display the interview.
   - Type up on a computer or write your article neatly.
   - Pin it to the school map you designed, in the room or place they work in.
   - Present in class or school assembly.

1.6 Project challenge

Project B: Write about an inspirational person you know in your community

Find out about someone you know.

1. Think about an inspirational person you know. It could be...
   - someone in your family
   - a teacher
   - a famous person.

2. Read this description about an inspirational person written by Maisie.

3. Answer these questions.
   a. Who is the person being described?
   b. What are his personal qualities?
   c. What do they enjoy doing together?
   d. How does he help Maisie and other young athletes?

4. Write your description about an inspirational person you know.

   Remember to:
   - write about why this person is special
   - write about their personal qualities
   - describe how they help and inspire others
   - write about similar interests you have or activities you do together
   - do a presentation about your inspirational person (use photos, articles and objects).

> My inspirational person is my dad.
>
> He's a kind, caring person who always does nice things for his family.
>
> My dad helps me to do my homework. He makes me feel better if I don't feel well or if I'm worried about something.
>
> I enjoy playing sport with my dad too. We're both really keen on running. We train together at the local athletics club where he coaches young athletes. He's very good at it! He motivates us to train hard, but he makes it fun for us all. We're a team and we work together!

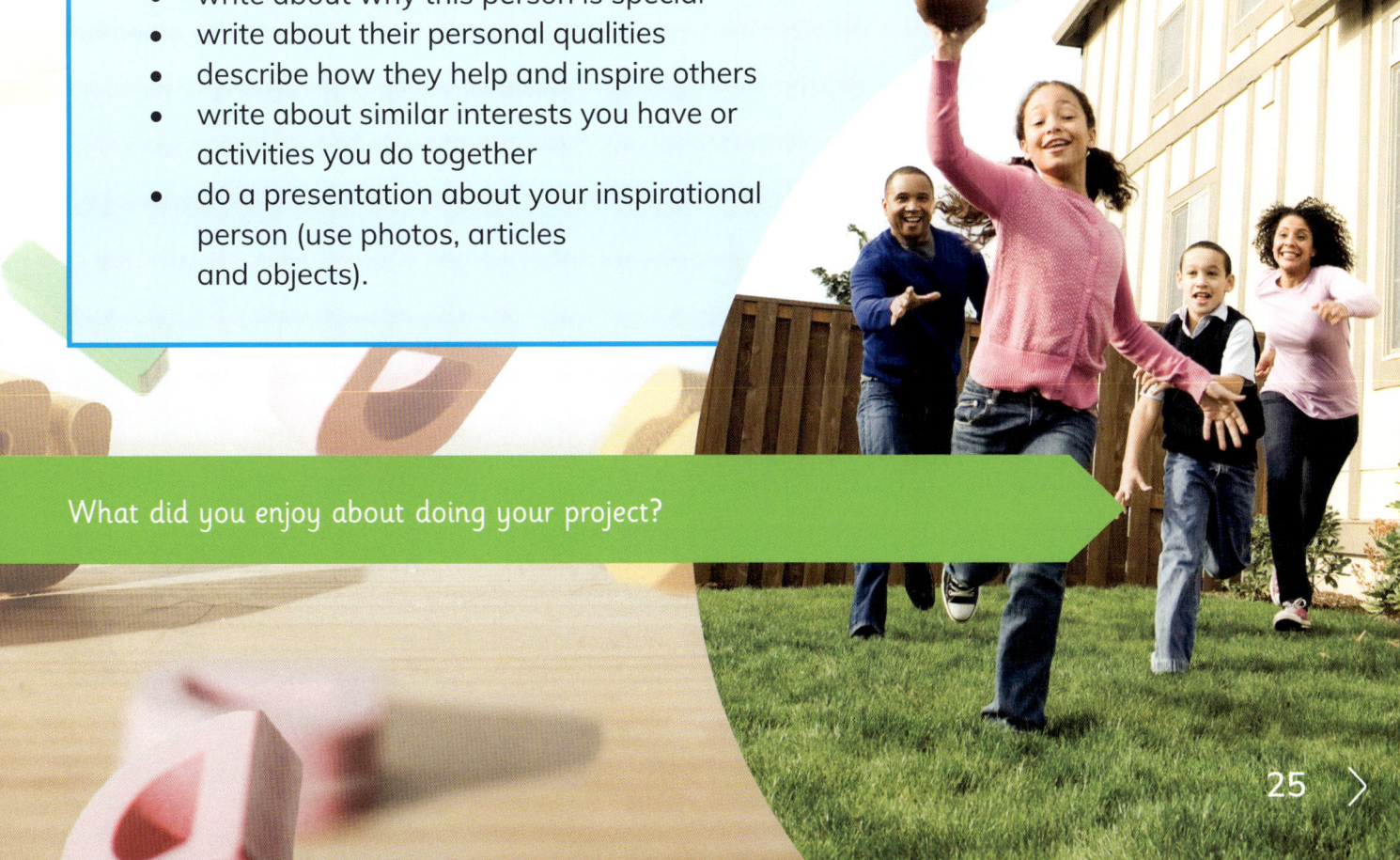

What did you enjoy about doing your project?

1 Our community

> 1.7 What do you know now?

What is a community?

1 How many parts of a community can you think of? Complete the list:
my family, _____, _____, _____.

2 How do these people help in a community?
parents   caretaker   firefighter   street cleaner   vet   football coach

3 Make sentences about yourself and your family using these verbs:
want   like   love   hope   enjoy

4 Which event in lesson 1.4 would you like to go to? Explain why.
I'd like to go to the _____ because _____.

5 Which people are 'the treasures' in the story in lesson 1.5?

6 Tell your partner about how you help in class. Use adverbs of frequency:
never   hardly ever   sometimes   usually   always

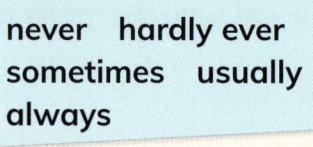

Look what I can do!

Write or show examples in your notebook.

I can talk about why families are special.

I can understand an article about an inspirational sports player.

I can ask questions to find out general information about school helpers and their jobs.

I can write a leaflet about an event in my community.

I enjoyed a story about special people in *The Treasure*.

I can write about a school helper or an inspirational person I know.

2 Earth and beyond

We are going to...

- **use** comparative and superlative adjectives to talk about the Earth's natural landscapes
- **explore** our solar system
- **describe** natural events
- **write a fact file** about a spacecraft
- **read** and enjoy a poem about Pluto
- **create a project** with a planet Earth or space theme.

Getting started

What can we discover on planet Earth and in our solar system?

a Look at the photo of Earth. What can you see?
b What can you see around Earth?
c How do you think this photo was taken?

Watch this!

2 Earth and beyond

> 2.1 Planet Earth

We are going to...
- compare Earth's natural landscapes.

1 **Talk:** In pairs, look at the pictures below. Which landscapes can you find in your country?

a b c
d e f

2 **Vocabulary:** Choose the adjectives to describe these landscapes.

| long | high | hot | freezing | icy | ~~dry~~ | huge |
| wide | wet | beautiful | humid | cool | warm |

The desert	The tropical rainforest	The Arctic	The mountains
dry			

3 **Listen** and check. Which of the places above are described? How do you know?

28

2.1 Think about it

4 Listen again and choose the correct answer.

1 The Amazon river is
   a 11 km long.
   b 6400 km long.
   c longer than the Nile.

2 The Sahara Desert is
   a one of four deserts in Africa.
   b hotter than the Kalahari Desert.
   c older than the Namib Desert.

3 The Kilauea volcano
   a erupts very often.
   b is bigger than the Mauna Loa volcano.
   c isn't colourful.

5 **Use of English:** Use the Language detective and the adjectives in Activity 2 to describe the pictures in Activity 1.

The Sahara is drier than the Amazon rainforest.

6 **Write** a **true** / **false** quiz about your country. Write six sentences.

Think about mountains, beaches, forests, deserts, the temperature.

Use comparative adjectives. Make sure some are true and some are false.

7 **Talk:** Do the quiz in groups of four, taking turns to ask and answer questions.

Listening tip

Listen for specific information

Before you listen, read the questions carefully and try to guess the answers.

First listen out for the answers and then listen again to find out more information. Guess any answers you don't know.

Language detective – Comparatives

The Namib Desert is **older than** the Sahara.
The Nile river is **longer than** the Amazon.
Is it **more dangerous** than you think?

- **Adjectives ending in –e add –r:**

  The Amazon is **wider than** the Nile.

- **Adjectives ending in –y change to –ier:**

  The Sahara is **drier than** the Namib Desert.

- **Double letters:**

  The Sahara is **hotter than** the Namib Desert.

2 Earth and beyond

> 2.2 Planets and orbits

We are going to...
- explore our solar system.

1 Test yourself with this quiz.

1. How many planets are there in our solar system?
   - a 8
   - b 9
   - c 10

2. These letters list the order of the planets from nearest to furthest from the Sun. Can you name them?

   M V E M J S U N

3. Is Pluto a planet?

4. What **orbits** the Sun?
   - a the Moon
   - b the universe
   - c Earth

5. What is another name for the Moon?
   - a Ceres
   - b Luna
   - c Saturn

6. How long does it take for the Moon to orbit Earth?
   - a more than 28 days
   - b less than 28 days
   - c more than 12 months

07 **2 Read and listen** to the introduction to the text about the solar system and check your answers.

08 **3 Read and listen** to the rest of the text. Complete notes about each planet.

4 Talk: Look at the Language detective. Ask and answer five questions about the planets and the solar system.

> Which is the smallest planet?

> The smallest planet is ____.

Language detective – Superlatives

- Short adjectives and long adjectives:

  Mercury is **the nearest** planet to the Sun.
  Saturn is one of the **most beautiful** planets.

- Adjectives ending in –y:

  Mars is one of **the driest** planets.

30

2.2 Science

In our solar system, eight planets move around the Sun. The nearest planet to the Sun is Mercury, followed by Venus, Earth, Mars, Jupiter, Saturn, Uranus and Neptune. Scientists used to think Pluto was a planet, but it is now called a dwarf planet because it is so small. There are four other known dwarf planets.

The Sun is in the middle of the solar system and the planets **orbit** it. Earth takes 12 months to orbit the Sun. Earth has one moon, which is sometimes called Luna by astronomers, that takes less than 28 days to travel around Earth.

Jupiter is 318 times bigger than Earth!

Neptune is the fourth largest of the eight planets.

New moons are **discovered** every year for Jupiter, Saturn, Uranus and Neptune!

Neptune has winds that travel at 2,000 km per hour!

Venus has **poisonous** yellow clouds.

Mercury is the smallest planet in our solar system and is the nearest planet to the Sun. It is grey and rocky. Mercury doesn't have any moons.

Earth is small and rocky and is the only planet to **support** life. Satellite pictures show that it is light blue with white clouds. Earth has one moon.

Mars is a red-orange colour. It is small, rocky and lifeless. It is also one of the driest planets. It has two small moons called Phobos and Deimos.

Saturn is pale yellow. It's famous for its thousands of bright rings and is one of the most beautiful planets in the solar system. Saturn has 62 moons (at least) – more than any other planet!

Key words: Science

orbit: travel around an object in space
discover: find out information
poisonous: very harmful
support: make something possible

2 Earth and beyond

2.3 Natural miracles

We are going to...
- **describe natural events.**

1 **Vocabulary:** Which natural events have you seen? Where? Match the words to the photos.

> northern lights   rainbow   lightning
> constellation   sunset

2 Do you know how these events happen? Write the correct word in the spaces.

a _____ happen when there is sunshine straight after rain.

b _____ happens when cold and warm air make electricity.

c _____ happen when the Sun goes down at the end of the day.

d _____ appear at night but they are caused by activity from the Sun.

e You can see _____ more easily in places where there are no city lights.

3 **Listen** to Zak describing his experience. Which photo from Activity 1 is he describing?

2.3 Talk about it

4 Listen again. Put the sentences in the order you hear them.

a I can see bright green lights… _____
b Here we are in Iceland. ___1___
c This is the most amazing thing I've ever seen! _____
d Now we're standing looking at the sky. _____
e The lights are moving and shaking! _____
f We're driving in the countryside to see something very special. _____

5 Find the examples of the present continuous in the sentences in Activity 4.

6 **Pronunciation:** Listen and repeat the sentences. Which words are contracted? What are they short for?

> **Language focus – Present continuous**
>
> We use the **present continuous** (be + verb + ing) to talk about things happening at the same time.

7 **Word study:** Work in pairs.

a Divide the descriptive words below into adjectives and verbs.

b Match the adjectives to the photos in Activity 1. Act out the verbs!

purple   special   dark   green   dance   amazing   bright
rise   pink   shake   blue   wave   jump   red

8 **Talk:** Work in pairs. Imagine you are experiencing one of the natural events in Activity 1 and create a commentary.

Use descriptive words and say …

- where you are
- why you are there
- what's happening
- how you feel.

9 Act out your commentary. Can your classmates guess where you are?

> Here we are in the…

> We are looking for…

2 Earth and beyond

2.4 Finding out about space technology

We are going to...
- write a fact file about a spacecraft.

1 **Talk:** In pairs, look at the photos. What do you know about space technology? Match the photos to the correct sentences.

a   A **satellite** orbits another planet to collect information.

b   Scientists can see planets and stars close up through a **telescope**.

c   A **space shuttle** can travel into space and come back again.

d   A **rover** can move across the surface of a planet or moon.

2 **Read** the fact file and match the headings to the sentences. Use the underlined words to help you.

| Size | What is it? |
| Amazing fact | What does it do? |

Fact file: A space shuttle — Fact file heading

1 A space shuttle <u>is</u> a rocket that travels into space and comes back to Earth again. It <u>is</u> extremely powerful and very, very fast.

2 It takes astronauts and scientists into space <u>to discover new information</u> about our solar system. It <u>can</u> also take other machines into space, for example rovers to Mars.

3 A space shuttle is <u>huge</u>! It is about <u>56</u> metres long. That's the same as nearly <u>five</u> school buses!

4 A space shuttle can reach a speed of more than 27 000 kilometres per hour! How <u>amazing</u> is that?

Use present simple to write facts

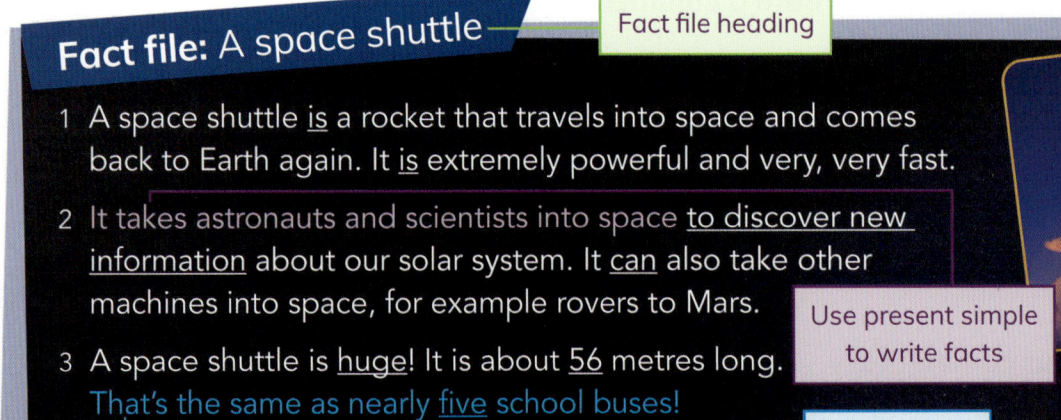

Picture

Interesting facts

2.4 Write about it

3. Circle all the information in the fact file that you didn't know before. In pairs, discuss which fact you think is the most interesting.

4. What do you know about the planet Mars? How do you think the Mars rover helps scientists find information about Mars?

5. Write a fact file about a Mars rover. Use the fact file in Activity 2 to help you. Follow these steps to help you find the information you need.

> **Language focus – Present simple**
>
> Use the present simple to describe facts. Remember to add 's' for **he**, **she** and **it**.
>
> *It takes astronauts and scientists into space...*

Research

Step 1:	Use the internet, books and magazines to find out information about the Mars rovers.
Step 2:	If you research online, ask your teacher which sites to use.
Step 3:	Use the fact file headings to help you find information.
Step 4:	Look for key words to help you find the right information.
Step 5:	If you work in a group, research a heading each. Then write the fact file together.

6. Present, display or publish your work.

2 Earth and beyond

2.5 Not a planet anymore

We are going to...
- read a poem about Pluto.

1 **Talk:** What do you know about Pluto? In pairs, talk about why you think the poem is called *Not a planet anymore*.

2 **Read and listen** to the poem. Look at the pictures. Is Pluto a happy planet? Why not?

Reading tip

Reading for gist

Read the poem and look at the pictures. Try to get a general idea of the meaning. Don't worry about words you don't know.

Not a Planet Anymore

by Joshua Seigal

All my life I've felt left out –
A tiny speck so far away.
The bigger kids won't let me play,
And now they say they have their doubt

5   That I am even one of them.
They are big and brave and bold
And I am tiny; blue and cold;
They are wondrous shiny gems.

And they don't want the likes of me.
10   They all have their moons and things;
Saturn has her lovely rings
And planet Earth has azure seas.

Yes, all my life I've felt left out.
My heart is big, my body small
15   And all my life I've longed to call:
'I AM PLUTO! HEAR MY SHOUT!'

2 Earth and beyond

3 Word study: Read and listen to the poem again. Look at the words in blue in the text and match them to the meanings a–e.

a   jewels
b   not sure about something
c   not included
d   a very small mark
e   wanted very much (for a long time)

4 Work in pairs. Think of synonyms for these adjectives from the poem.

tiny   bold   wondrous   azure

5 Read the poem again and answer the questions.

a   Is Pluto near or a long way from the Sun?
    Which line in the poem tells us?
b   Who do you think 'the bigger kids' are?
c   How do 'the bigger kids' make Pluto feel? Why?
d   Find words to describe Pluto and the other planets.
    What differences do you notice?
e   What does Pluto want to do?

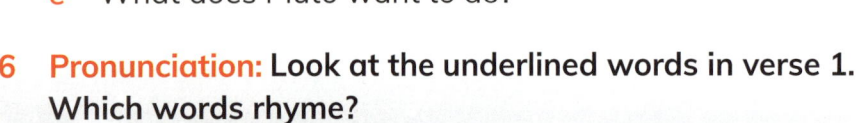

6 Pronunciation: Look at the underlined words in verse 1. Which words rhyme?

Find the rhyming words in the other verses.
Which is the sound that is the same in each case?

2.5 Read and respond

7 **Talk:** **Did you like this poem? What did you like about it?**

Do you have a favourite poem?

Does it rhyme? If so, how does it rhyme?

I really liked this poem, but my favourite poem is…

8 **In the poem, Pluto has a 'voice' and a personality. Which is your favourite planet? Why?**

- Think of adjectives and short phrases to describe your favourite planet. What is its personality like?
- Draw and colour your favourite planet.
- Label it with descriptive words and phrases.
- Describe it to your partner.

   This is Mars. It is warm and red. I think it is a strong planet but it can sometimes be angry…

9 **Values:** **Including the people around us**

In the poem, Pluto says that it feels 'left out'. Talk about the questions in small groups.

a   How do you think it feels to be left out?
b   What situations can make us feel left out?
c   What can we do to make each other feel included?

2 Earth and beyond

> 2.6 Project challenge

Project A: Create your own adjective poem

1. **Read the poem below and underline all the adjectives.**

   How many adjectives are there on each line? What shape is the poem?

   > The
   > Arctic
   > Frozen, snowy,
   > Huge, icy, bright,
   > Beautiful home for polar bears
   > and penguins,
   > Sparkling, white,
   > The mysterious
   > Arctic.

2. Choose a subject from these topics. Write down adjectives and other words connected to the subject (for example, animals, weather, plants, trees, natural features).

   beautiful landscapes

   the solar system

   planets

3. Use the poem above to help you write your own poem.

4. Decorate your poem with pictures and display it. Find pictures online or in magazines, or draw your own.

5. Read your classmates' poems. Make a note of new adjectives and ideas about the other subjects.

2.6 Project challenge

Project B: Design your own space shuttle

Find out about how astronauts prepare for space.

1. Work in pairs or small groups. Why do astronauts travel into space? Work together and write down all the reasons.

2. How does an astronaut prepare to travel into space? What things does he or she need for the journey? Think about food, clothing, equipment, entertainment and daily routine.

3. Imagine you are an astronaut preparing for a journey into space. Answer these questions with your group.
   a. Why are you travelling into space?
   b. How many of you are going on the journey?
   c. How long will you be in space?
   d. What do you need to take with you?

4. Design a space shuttle for your space journey. Draw and label its special parts and give your shuttle a name. Use your answers to question 3 to help you.

5. Imagine you are taking off in your space shuttle. What can you see as you leave Earth? Write a short commentary. Use interesting adjectives.

   Here we are in our space shuttle, (name).
   It is...
   We are travelling at _ km per hour!
   Out of the window we can see...

6. Type up your commentary and add to your design. Display your space shuttle project in your classroom.

What do you like about your project? What do you dislike?

2 Earth and beyond

> 2.7 What do you know now?

What can we discover on planet Earth and in our solar system?

1 How many different kinds of landscapes and natural places can you name?

2 Write five comparative sentences about landscapes, using the adjectives below.

> long   hot   dry
> old   active

3 Write a list of the planets from the nearest to the furthest from the Sun.

4 Which is the smallest planet and the nearest to the Sun? Which planet do you think is the most beautiful? Why?

5 Make some sentences to describe the northern lights in lesson 2.3. Use these words to help you.

> green   purple   dance
> wave   sky   bright

6 How do you think the photo on page 27 was taken?

7 Think about the poem in lesson 2.5. Why was Pluto sad?

Look what I can do!

Write or show examples in your notebook.

I can talk about natural landscapes using comparative adjectives.

I can identify the planets in our solar system.

I can describe planets using superlative adjectives.

I can describe some natural events.

I can write a fact file about a spacecraft.

I can understand a poem about Pluto.

I can identify words that rhyme.

3 Homes

Stadium

We are going to...
- **talk about** homes around the world
- **learn about** eco-houses and the material we need to build them
- **use modal verbs** and **yes/no questions** to talk about strange buildings
- **write a magazine article** about a famous place
- **read** and enjoy an extract from *The Hobbit*.

Supermarket

Hospital

Getting started

How are buildings important to us?

a Which buildings can you see in the picture?
b Which buildings do you have in your town or city? What are they used for?
c Think of a famous building or place in your town or city. Why is it special?

Watch this!

School

43

3 Homes

> 3.1 How can we describe where we live?

We are going to...
- talk about homes around the world.

1 **Vocabulary:** Read the clues and match them to the numbered parts of the house.

   a   You can see through this!
   b   It's at the top!
   c   You eat here!
   d   I sleep here. I'm tired!
   e   I watch the TV and play on my tablet/computer here.
   f   My family cook here.
   g   I wash here.

2   How are these houses different? Can you match the words with the pictures?

   stilt house   eco-house   apartment   bungalow   detached house   yurt

3 **Listen** to children describing their homes. Match the speakers to the photos in Activity 2.

3.1 Think about it

4   What do the children like about their homes? Read and match to the photos.
- He likes it because he loves nature and animals. __e__
- She likes it because you don't have to walk up and down the stairs. _____
- He loves it because it's got a lot of space. _____
- He likes it because it's modern and energy-efficient. _____
- He loves it because he likes fishing with his mum and dad. _____
- She loves it because it is near her school and it has great views. _____

5   **Talk:** Which house do you like best?

6   Describe your home to your partner. Why do you like it?

I live in a…   It's made of…   It's got… (four rooms)
It's…+ (adjective)   I love it/like because…

> I like the eco-house because it's modern.

7   Look at the photos in Activity 8. Which home would you like to live in? Why are these homes different to other homes?

8   **Word study:** Choose a word from the list to describe each photo. Think of more words too!

enormous   spacious   comfortable   relaxing   modern
grand   tiny   mysterious   wooden   colourful

a tree house
b houseboat
c castle

9   **Listen** to Sam talking about one of the photos in Activity 8. Answer the questions.
a   Which photo is he describing?
b   How does he describe it?
c   What's different about living here?

10 **Talk:** Which is your favourite place to live?
Tell your partner using the adjectives from the colourful words in Activity 8.

3 Homes

3.2 The eco-house

We are going to...
- learn about eco-houses and the material we need to build them.

1. What does eco- or ecological mean to you? What is an eco-house? Tick the pictures that belong to an eco-house.

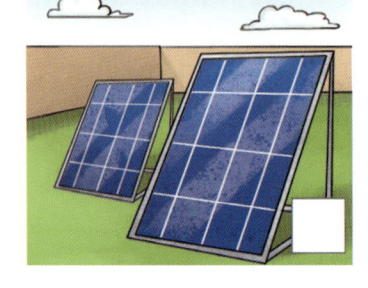

a b
c d

🎧 14 2 **Read and listen** to the text. What's good about an eco-house?

An eco-house

This 'earth shelter' house is built into the ground. It is made from recycled materials that the owners found in the **rubbish tip**. They used **local materials** like stone, metal, wood and mud too! The walls are made of stone and mud and they used wood to make the roof.

This eco-house uses natural resources like water and energy **efficiently**. It has a wood burner to heat the house and big windows to let in natural light. It also has solar panels to provide energy for heating and lighting, and earth and grass on top of the roof to keep the house warm. Outside, there is a large tub to collect water when it rains, and for watering the vegetable garden in the summer.

3.2 Ecology

Key words: Environment

rubbish: waste things that people don't need or want

rubbish tip: a place where people can throw away large pieces of rubbish

local materials: things that you can find nearby

efficiently: quick and well-organised

Language detective – Infinitive of purpose

They used wood **to make** the roof.

They have solar panels **to provide** energy.

3 **Use of English:** Cover up the reading text in Activity 2.
Complete the sentences using the correct infinitive of purpose from the box.

| to heat | to collect | to keep | to build |

a There are solar panels on the roof _____ the house.

b They also have grass on the roof _____ the house warm.

c They used mud and stone _____ the walls.

d They have a large water tub _____ rainwater.

4 Now read the text again to check your answers.

5 **Vocabulary:** Match the phrases to the correct pictures.

1 turn off lights

2 turn off appliances

3 put on a jumper

4 unplug charger

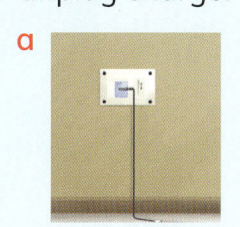

6 Which actions do you do most to save energy in your home?

47

3 Homes

3.3 Strange buildings

We are going to...
- use modal verbs and **yes/no** questions to talk about strange buildings.

1 **Talk:** Look at these photos of buildings. What's strange about them? Talk with a partner.

2 **Listen** to the children playing a guessing game. Which building do they describe?

It's made from books!

It looks like a shoe.

3.3 Talk about it

3 Pronunciation: Listen and repeat the yes/no questions below. Use the arrows to help you. Practise with a partner.

a Is it made from books? ↗
b Is it colourful? ↗
c Is it a bag shape? ↗
d Does it look like an upside-down house? ↗
e Does it have windows? ↗

Language focus

We form yes/no questions with an **auxiliary verb** (**be**, **do** or **have**). Circle the auxiliary verbs in the questions in Activity 3.

4 Talk: Play the guessing game with your partner. Take turns asking questions about the photos in Activity 1. Ask yes/no questions.

Is it colourful?

No, it isn't.

5 Use of English: Look and talk about what the buildings in Activity 1 might be.

Language detective – Modal verbs of possibility

It **can't** be a house.   It **might** be a museum.
It **could** be a library.   It **must** be a school.

0% ⟶ 100%
Not possible   Very possible

6 Check your ideas. Listen to the children talking about what the buildings are used for.

7 Listen to the dialogues again and circle the correct modal verb.

a It **could** / **can't** be a museum.
b I think photo 2 **could** / **must** be a factory.
c I think it **might** / **must** be a hotel because it's very big!
d It **could** / **can't** be a cool apartment building!
e It **can't** / **must** be a real house!
f It **must** / **might** be a library with all those books!

8 Find some photos of unusual buildings and find out what they are used for. Ask your partner their opinion. Use modal verbs.

*What do you think it **could** be?*

*It **might** be a school because I can see a playground.*

3 Homes

> 3.4 Famous places

We are going to…

- write a magazine article about a famous place.

Watch this!

1 **Talk:** There are famous buildings and landmarks all over the world. How many famous places are there where you live?

2 **Read** the magazine article and find the answers.

   a   Where is Machu Picchu?
   b   What was it?
   c   Who discovered it?
   d   How many ways can you travel to Machu Picchu?
   e   How would you like to travel there? Why?

My Famous Places: Peru: Machu Picchu

1 Machu Picchu, also known as **'The Lost Inca City', is in the Cusco region of Peru in South America.** It is high up in the mountains above the Urubamba River. —— Location

2 'Machu' means old or ancient and 'Picchu' means peak or mountain. It was built by the Inca emperor Pachacuti and historians think it was a spiritual and ceremonial Inca site. It was hidden from the world for centuries until an American explorer, **Hiram Bingham, discovered it in 1911.** —— Historical fact

3 There are different ways to travel to Machu Picchu – some are easier than others! **You can take the train from _____, you can fly in by helicopter or you can trek.** The Inca Trail is the most difficult way to get to the **mysterious** lost city of the Incas. It is the most famous trek in South America. It is 43 kilometres long and the trek goes through **beautiful** mountain scenery and **lush** forests until you arrive at the **spectacular** Inca site. You can choose an easy, moderate or difficult route, depending on how fit you are. **I think I'd choose the easy one…** What about you?

Travel information

Use interesting adjectives

Opinion

3.4 Write about it

3 **Write:** Choose one of these famous landmarks and write a magazine article about it. Follow the steps and use the model in Activity 2 to help you.

Step 1: Research	Use the internet, books and magazines to find out information on location, historical facts, travel information and things to see and do.
Step 2: Planning	Use paragraphs: 1 Location 2 Historical facts 3 Travel information
Step 3: Writing	Remember to use interesting adjectives: The trek goes through ~~nice~~ **beautiful** scenery.
Step 4: Read and check	Swap with a partner. Check for spelling mistakes!

The Prophet's Mosque, Saudi Arabia

The Taj Mahal, India

4 Present, display or publish your work.

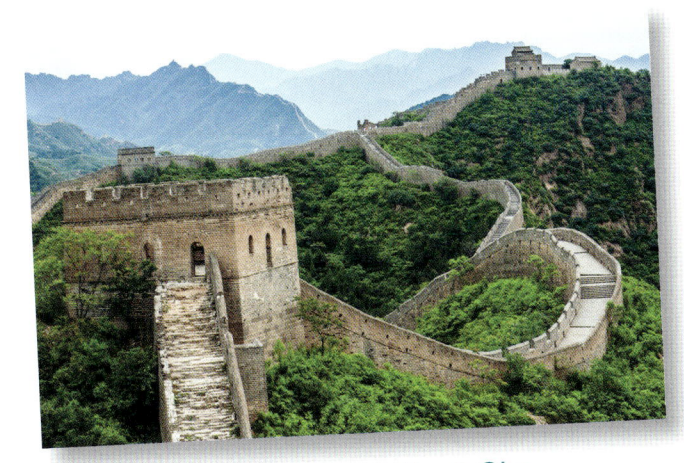

The Great Wall of China

The Colosseum, Italy

Writing tip

Paragraphs

Organise your writing into paragraphs, with clear information in each one.

51

3 Homes

> 3.5 The Hobbit

We are going to...

- read an extract from **The Hobbit**.

1 **Talk:** *The Hobbit* is a book by J.R.R. Tolkien. It is also a famous series of films. In this extract, we learn about the hobbit and his unusual home. Look at the pictures and answer the questions.

   a   Who do you think the hobbit is?
   b   What is his home like?

2 **Read** the extract from *The Hobbit*. Check your ideas from Activity 1 and match the headings to the correct paragraphs, 1, 2 and 3.

   a   What is a hobbit like?
   b   Description of a hobbit-hole
   c   The hobbit's house

The Hobbit
by J.R.R. Tolkien.

In a **hole** in the ground there lived a hobbit. Not a nasty, dirty, wet hole, filled with the ends of worms and an oozy smell, nor yet a dry, bare, sandy hole with nothing in it to sit down or to eat: it was a hobbit-hole, and that means **comfort**.

3 Read the story again. Are the sentences after each part **true** or **false**?

   a   The hobbit lives under the ground.   **true / false**
   b   His home is not nice to live in.   **true / false**

3.5 Read and respond

5   It had a perfectly round door like a porthole, painted green, with a shiny
    yellow brass knob in the exact middle. The door opened on to a tube-shaped
    hall like a **tunnel**: a very comfortable tunnel without smoke, with panelled
    walls, and floors tiled and carpeted, provided with polished chairs, and lots
    and lots of pegs for hats and coats – the hobbit was **fond of** visitors. The
10 tunnel wound on and on, going fairly but not quite straight into the side of
    the hill – The Hill, as all the people for many miles around called it – and
    many little round doors opened out of it, first on the one side and then on
    another. No going upstairs for the hobbit: bedrooms, bathrooms, cellars,
    pantries (lots of these), wardrobes (he had whole rooms devoted to clothes),
15 kitchens, dining-rooms, all were on the same floor, and indeed on the same
    passage. The best rooms were all on the left-hand side (going in), for these
    were the only ones to have windows, deep-set round windows looking over
    his garden, and **meadows** beyond, sloping down to the river.

c   The door looks like a window in a ship.   true / false
d   The hobbit's hall is very long and narrow.   true / false
e   His house has more than one floor.   true / false
f   You can't see outside from the hobbit's house.   true / false

3 Homes

This hobbit was a very well-to-do hobbit, and his name was Baggins. The Bagginses had lived in the neighbourhood of The Hill for time out of mind, and people considered them
20 very **respectable**, not only because most of them were rich, but also because they never had any adventures or did anything unexpected: you could tell what a Baggins would say on any question without the bother of asking him. This is a story of how a Baggins had an adventure, and found himself doing
25 and saying things altogether unexpected. He may have lost the neighbours' respect, but he gained – well, you will see whether he gained anything in the end.

g The hobbit, Baggins, comes from a poor family. true / false
h People thought the Baggins family were responsible and well-behaved. true / false
i The Baggins family never did crazy, dangerous things. true / false
j One day, something unusual and exciting happened to Baggins. true / false

3.5 Read and respond

4 Look at the sentences under each part of the extract again.
Correct the false sentences.

5 Word study: Find the words in blue in the story and match to the meanings below.

a a good person
b pretty fields
c an open place in the ground
d like very much
e an easy and nice feeling
f a long passage through the ground

6 Read the story again and answer the questions.

a Find a word to describe the hobbit-hole.
b What rooms does the house have?
c What is good about the rooms on the left-hand side?
d How long have the Baggins family lived on The Hill?
e Why is it surprising that Baggins has an adventure?

7 In pairs, talk about the questions.

a Would you like to live in this house? Why? Why not?
b Which of your ideas from Activity 1 did you find in the text?
c *The Hobbit* is a book and a series of films. What do you know about them?

8 Values: Making visitors welcome

In *The Hobbit*, we learn that the hobbit 'was fond of visitors'.

a What did Baggins do to make people welcome in his home?
b What other things can you do to make visitors welcome in your home or school?
c How often do you visit other homes or schools? What do people do to make you feel welcome?

55

3 Homes

> 3.6 Project challenge

Project A: Create a dream home!

1. **What is your dream home like?**
   - Close your eyes and imagine your dream home. What kind of building is it? Where is it? Why do you like it? Give reasons.
   - Plan and write your ideas in a mind map.

2. **Describe your dream home.**

   What is it made of?
   What special features does it have?
   Add your ideas to your mind map.

3. **Write about your dream home.**

   Use the ideas in your plan/mind map and the sentence prompts to help you. Write and check your description.

4. **Create a picture of your dream home. Label its special features.**

   It is made of stone and glass.

   It has a swimming pool with a water slide!

   This is my dream home.
   It is a _____.
   It is made of _____.
   It has got a _____.
   It has a _____ to _____.
   I love it because _____.

5. **Display your dream home project in your classroom.**

   Read about your classmates' dream homes.
   Ask questions!

3.6 Project challenge

Project B: Describe an interesting building in your town or city

1. **Find out about interesting buildings in your town or city.**

    Work in pairs or in a small group. Use the internet, go to the library or talk to your family about buildings.

2. **Choose a building and write five interesting facts about it.**
    - What does it look like? What is it made of?
    - Where is it?
    - How can you travel to it?

3. **Write about its history.**
    - Who built it?
    - Why is it special?

4. **Draw a picture or take a photo of your building. Add your interesting facts and make a poster.**

5. **Talk about your building to your partner or group.**
    - Play a guessing game! Ask your partner or group to guess your building (hide the picture). Answer **yes** or **no**.

    Is it made of concrete?

    Does it have a flag?

    No, it isn't.

    Yes, it does.

    - Show your partner or group the picture and tell them interesting facts about your building. Give reasons why it is important to you.

How would you improve your project?

3 Homes

> 3.7 What do you know now?

How are buildings important to us?

1 Make a list of types of buildings in your town or city. Why are they important? Which ones do you visit the most?

2 Write the names of five types of house. Which one do you like best? Why? Tell your partner.

I like apartments best because you can see views of the city.

3 What materials can you use to build a house or building? What is your home made of?

4 What special features does an eco-house have? Discuss with a partner.

It has solar panels to heat the house.

5 Tell your partner some ways to save energy at home. Which ones do you do?

I always turn off lights if no one is in the room.

6 Think of famous buildings in your country. Choose one and write some interesting adjectives to describe it.

Look what I can do!

Write or show examples in your notebook.

I can talk about different types of home.

I can describe an eco-house.

I can identify the materials used to build a house.

I can talk about ways to save energy at home.

I can use modal verbs and yes/no questions to talk about buildings.

I can write about famous landmarks in my town or country.

I can understand an extract from *The Hobbit*.

Check your progress 1

1 **Read the clues and guess the words.**

   a This person is your mother's father.
   b This adjective means very, very cold.
   c This rocket can travel into space and come back again.
   d This adjective describes a house with lots of space.
   e This type of house has only one floor and no stairs.
   f This person cleans and fixes things in your school.
   g This machine can move across the surfaces of planets and moons.
   h This is a sport you can do in the sea.
   i This type of home is in the same building as other homes.

2 **Now add one word to each vocabulary group in Activity 1.**

   a grandfather, cousin

3 **Play Bingo! Choose six words and write them in a grid like the one below.**

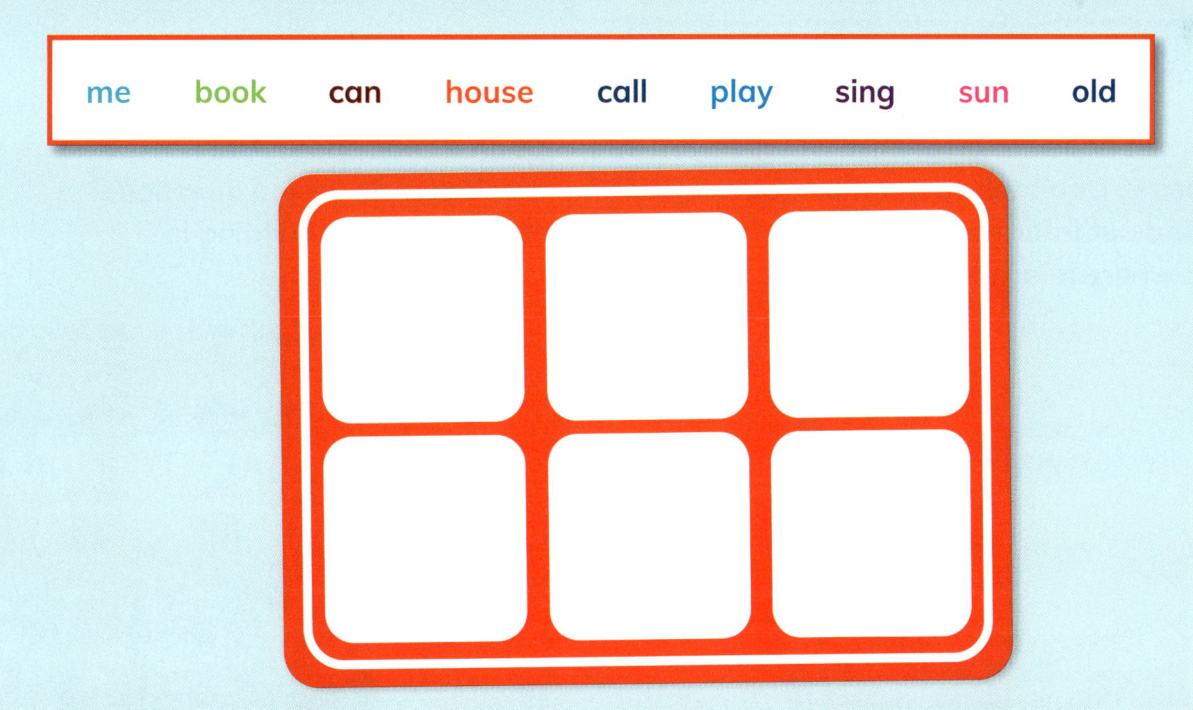

| me | book | can | house | call | play | sing | sun | old |

4 **Listen to your teacher. Cross out the words that rhyme in your grid. When you have crossed out all of your words, say 'Bingo!'**

Check your progress 1

5 Work in pairs. Each sentence has an error. Take turns to roll a dice and choose the sentence with the same number. Can you correct the errors?

1. My school is big than my cousin's school.
2. There is a large water tub in our school collect rainwater.
3. My country has the taller mountains in the world.
4. My friends really enjoy play basketball.
5. When I am older I want be a P.E. teacher.
6. The building opposite our school must be a library – I'm not sure.

6 Read the corrected sentences from Activity 5 and tick (✓) the ones that are true for you. Compare with your partner. Which ones are the same?

7 In groups, write a quiz! Choose from these topics. Write questions for your classmates to find answers in Units 1–3.

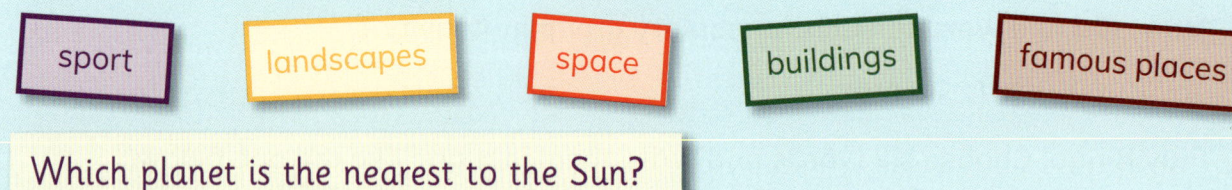

sport   landscapes   space   buildings   famous places

Which planet is the nearest to the Sun?

8 Swap quizzes. Which group got the most correct answers?

9 Work in pairs. Your teacher will give you information about photo A or photo B. Don't tell each other! Your partner must ask you six yes/no questions to find out information about your photo, then guess what the building is and where it is in the world.

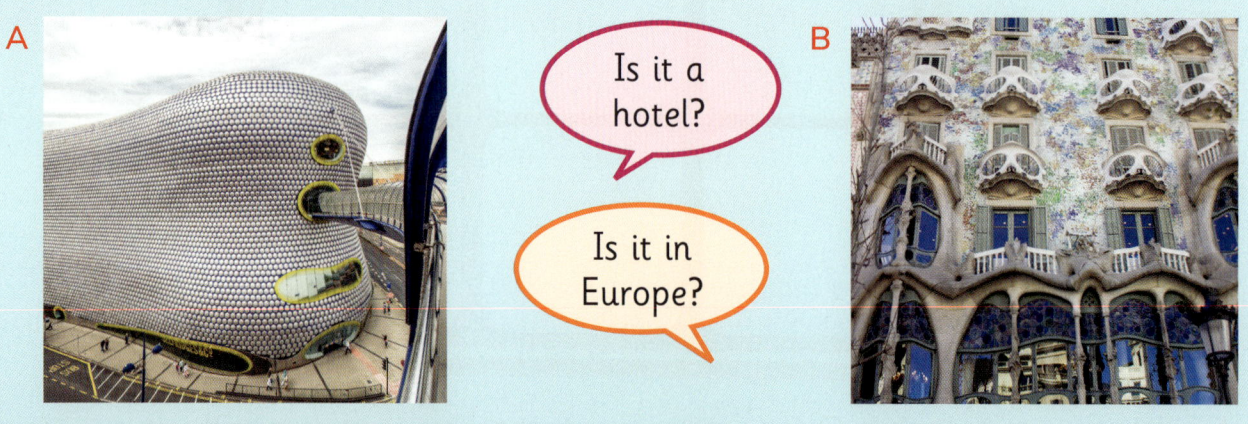

Is it a hotel?

Is it in Europe?

10 Compare the stories and poems in Units 1, 2 and 3. Which one did you like best? Why?

I liked… because…

4 Food

We are going to...

- **discover** what children eat for breakfast around the world
- **find out** how chocolate is made
- **write about** quantities of things
- **explain** how to grow a vegetable using connecting words
- **write** a poem about a fruit
- **enjoy** a story about a special cake.

Getting started

What can we discover about food?

a Look at the photo of people enjoying food. Which types of food can you see?
b What kind of food do you like? Why? How does food make you feel?
c Where do you think the food you eat comes from?

Watch this!

4 Food

> 4.1 Do we all eat the same breakfast?

We are going to...
- discover what children eat for breakfast around the world.

1 **Vocabulary:** In pairs, read the names of the foods. Can you find them in the photos below? Which picture do you see the food in: a, b, c or d?

cheese _____a_____
bread _____
banana _____
orange juice _____
chicken _____
onions _____
mushrooms _____
tomatoes _____
egg _____
papaya _____

2 Do you eat the same or similar food in your country? Discuss in pairs.

We don't eat much cheese.

No, but we eat a lot of fruit, like papaya.

3 **Listen** and match the children to the food from Activity 1 that they eat for breakfast.

a Lucas

b Nehir

c Kuong

62

4.1 Think about it

4 **Word study:** How does our food grow? Match the plant or tree to the correct fruit or vegetable. Do they all grow in your country?

1 2 3 4 5

a b c d e

5 Look at the pictures in Activity 4 again and answer **true** or **false**.

a A tomato grows on a tree.   true / false

b A mushroom grows on a plant.   true / false

c A banana grows on a tree.   true / false

d A papaya grows on the ground.   true / false

e An onion grows on a plant.   true / false

6 **Use of English:** Read the Language detective describing the food in the photo.

Write two more positive and negative sentences about the photo.

Language detective – Some and any		
Positive sentences	**Negative sentences**	**Questions**
There is **some** jam.	There isn't **any** soup.	Is there **any** bread?
There are **some** oranges.	There aren't **any** vegetables.	Are there **any** grapes?

7 What do you eat for breakfast?

- Draw a picture and label the food and drink. Write your name on the picture.
- Get into groups. Put all the pictures in the middle of the table.
- Take turns to choose a picture. Don't tell your classmates which one! Your classmates ask you questions and guess whose breakfast you are describing.

4 Food

4.2 All about chocolate!

We are going to...
- find out about where chocolate comes from
- write about quantities of things.

Reading tip

Using pictures

Look at the pictures around a text to help you understand what it is about.

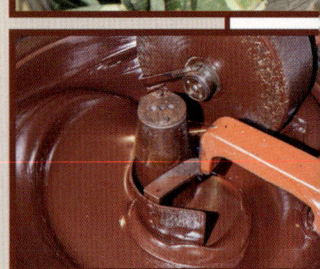

1 **Talk** in pairs. Answer the questions.
   a   What is your favourite kind of chocolate?
   b   Do you know what chocolate is made of? How is it made?
   c   When was the first chocolate bar invented?
   d   Why does chocolate melt in our mouths?

2 **Read and listen** to the text. Check your answers to Activity 1. Use the photos to help you.

From bean to bar!

The first chocolate bar was invented by Joseph Fry in 1847.

Growing
Chocolate is made from cacao beans, which grow on a tropical tree called *Theobroma cacao*. Cacao is grown in warm tropical countries close to the equator. A lot of cacao beans are grown in Central and South America.

Collecting the beans
The beans are usually harvested twice a year. They grow in pods on the tree and the workers use big knives called machetes to cut down the pods. They open the pods with their hands so that the beans inside don't break.

Preparing the beans
The beans are put into wooden containers. The containers are covered with banana leaves and left for a week. Then the beans travel to factories where they are turned into chocolate.

Making the beans into chocolate
Making the chocolate is difficult in hot countries, so the factories are usually in cooler countries, in Europe or North America. Here the cacao beans are roasted in big ovens. Then the beans are crushed into a paste. Plenty of sugar, cocoa butter, milk and a little vanilla are mixed together to make the paste sweet. Then the mixture is cooled and we have chocolate!

Product
Did you know that there are over 500 varieties of chocolate? Most chocolate is used in bars, cakes and desserts, but a few varieties are used in meat, chilli and pasta dishes too. There are few sweets as popular as chocolate!

Chocolate melts in our mouth because the melting point of cocoa butter is lower than the temperature of the human body.

4.2 Geography

3 Read the text again. Are these sentences **true** or **false**?

a	Cacao beans are grown in hot countries.	true / false
b	Cacao beans are harvested once a year.	true / false
c	The workers use big knives called machetes to open the pods.	true / false
d	The chocolate is made in hot countries.	true / false
e	Sugar is mixed into the paste so that it is sweet.	true / false
f	When the mixture is heated we have the final product.	true / false

Language focus

We use sentences with **is/are** + past participle to describe a process:

Chocolate is made from cacao beans...

4 Underline all the information in the text that you didn't know before.
Which fact did you think was the most interesting? Compare with your partner.

Language detective – Quantifiers

- Countable / Uncountable nouns: **a lot of / plenty of**
- Countable nouns: **few / a few**
- Uncountable nouns: **little / a little**

5 Find and underline examples of the quantifiers in the text on page 64.

6 **Use of English:** Circle the correct quantifier in each sentence.
Look at the nouns first. Are they countable or uncountable?

a There are **plenty of** / **a few** meat dishes with chocolate but not many.

b **A little** / **Few** people don't like chocolate!

c **A lot of** / **Few** sugar is mixed with the cacao paste and a **little** / **few** vanilla.

d **A little** / **few** chocolate is fine but too much is bad for your teeth!

7 **Write:** Choose one of these foods (or one of your own) to write about.
Find out information on the internet or in a library.

| tea | coffee | bread | sugar |

Which plant does it come from? What is the climate?
How does it grow? How do people make it?

Find a picture of your product and display with the process.

4 Food

> 4.3 Grow your own!

We are going to...

- explain how to grow a vegetable using connecting words.

1 **Talk:** How do they grow? In pairs, try this quick quiz.

1. Which vegetable grows under the ground?
   - a tomatoes
   - b carrots
2. Which vegetables grow on the ground?
   - a cabbages
   - b potatoes
3. Which vegetables grow high up the plant?
   - a courgettes
   - b okra
4. Which fruit grows in a tree?
   - a watermelons
   - b mangoes
5. Which fruit or vegetable can you grow without soil?
   - a onion
   - b cress
6. Why do you think people grow their own fruit and vegetables?

2 Find these objects in the pictures a–f. Which vegetable is being grown?

cotton wool | a plastic bottle | a paper towel | plastic container | coloured pens | seeds

4.3 Talk about it

3   **Listen** to Rosa describing how to grow a vegetable. Put the pictures in Activity 2 in order from 1 to 6. Why has a smiley face been drawn?

4   Put the sentence parts in the correct order. Listen again and check.

   a   Then put water on a paper towel... _____
   b   Before you start, clean a recycled plastic pot... _____
   c   When there are green leaves on your cress plant you can eat them! _____
   d   Then draw a face on it with coloured pen... _____
   e   After that, put water on some cotton wool... _____

5   **Word study:** Check the meaning of the verbs in a dictionary. In pairs, take it in turns to act out the groups of words below.

   grow a plant   **clean** the container   **rinse** with water
   press the seeds   **fold** the paper towel   **cut** the top off

6   **Pronunciation:** Listen and underline the word that is weak or that you don't hear in each sentence.

   a   Grow it in your classroom...
   b   Before you start...
   c   ...rinse with water...
   d   ...press them down...
   e   ...put your pot...
   f   ...ask an adult...

   Speaking tip

   Linking words together when you speak makes you sound more natural!

7   **Talk:** Can you remember how to grow a cress plant? Work in pairs and describe how to do it. Use the pictures in Activity 2, the connecting words, and the words from Activity 5 to help you.

   Before you start, clean a....

   Then draw a face...

   Language focus – Connectives

   We use the connecting words **before**, **when**, **then** and **after that** to show the order that something happens.

8   Which fruit and vegetables do you like? Have you ever grown a fruit or vegetable plant? How did you grow it?

4 Food

> 4.4 A fruit poem

We are going to...

- write a poem about a fruit.

1 Talk: Work in pairs and talk about the questions.

a   What does an **apple** look like?
b   How does it smell?
c   How does it taste?
d   How does it feel?
e   How does it sound?

2 Read and listen to the 'Apple' poem. Check your ideas from Activity 1.

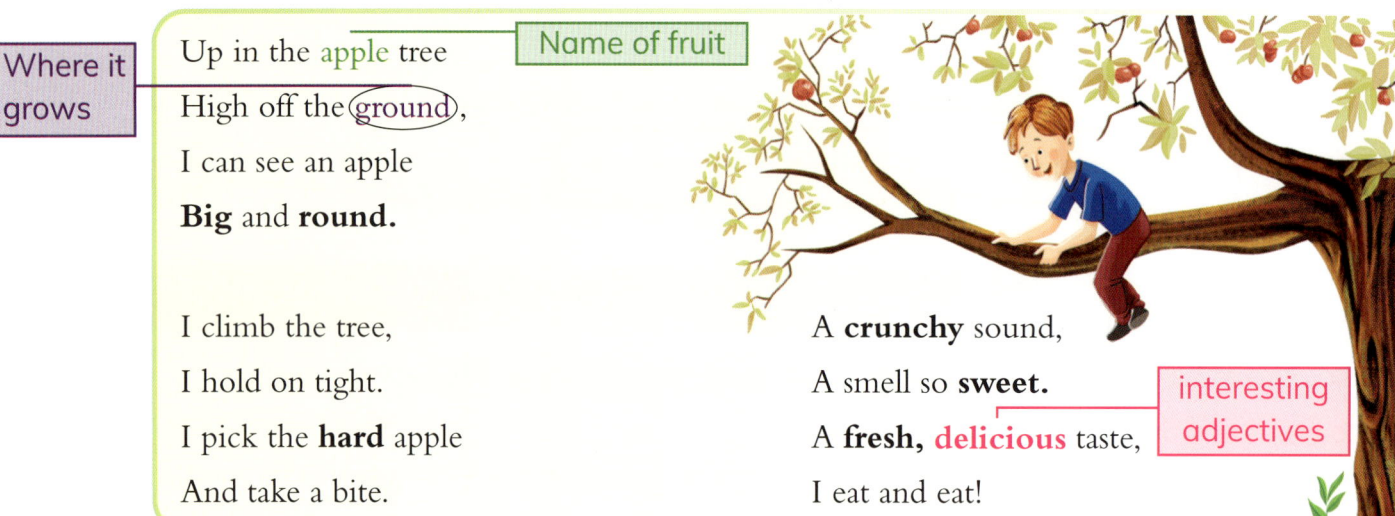

Where it grows → Up in the apple tree
High off the (ground),
I can see an apple
Big and **round**.

Name of fruit

I climb the tree,
I hold on tight.
I pick the **hard** apple
And take a bite.

A **crunchy** sound,
A smell so **sweet**.
A **fresh, delicious** taste,
I eat and eat!

interesting adjectives

3 Pronunciation: Listen again and circle two words that rhyme in each verse.

The rhyming words in verse 1 are **ground** and...

4 Vocabulary: Write the adjectives that describe the apple in the correct column. Some adjectives can go in more than 1 column. Which adjective do you like best? Explain why you like it to your partner.

The senses				
Sight	Touch	Smell	Taste	Hear
big	big			

68

4.4 Write about it

5 Find the meaning of these adjectives and write them in the correct column in Activity 4.

| juicy | salty | smooth | creamy | spicy | chewy | long |
| large | spiky | bitter | soft | crispy | sticky | colourful |

6 Read the sentences and choose the best adjective.
   a   The durian fruit looks **spiky** / **smooth**.
   b   The raspberry feels **hard** / **soft**.
   c   The dragon fruit looks **long** / **colourful**.
   d   The pineapple tastes **sweet** / **spicy**.
   e   The papaya tastes **salty** / **juicy**.

raspberry   dragon fruit
papaya   pineapple   durian

7 **Write** a poem about a fruit grown in your country. Follow the steps below to help you.

Step 1: Research	Choose a fruit that grows in your country. • Where does it grow? • Does it grow in a particular region of your country? • Does it grow on a tree or a plant?
Step 2: Planning	Decide which adjectives best describe your fruit. • What does it look/taste/smell/feel like? • Does it make a sound when you eat it? • Why do you like it?
Step 3: Writing	Draw a template in the shape of your fruit. Write your poem in it.
Step 4: Read	Listen to the rhyming words. Compliment each other: *It's really good! I like your poem!*

8 Read your poems aloud in small groups. Display or publish your work.

4 Food

4.5 Charlie and the Chocolate Factory

We are going to...
- enjoy a story about a magical chocolate factory.

1 **Talk:** Would you like to visit a chocolate or sweet factory? What do you think it would be like inside?

2 **Read and listen** to the first extract from the story, introducing Charlie and his family. Answer the questions.

Charlie and the Chocolate Factory
by Roald Dahl

Charlie and his family

Charlie Bucket was a young boy who lived with all his family (six grown-ups) in a small wooden house on the edge of a great town.

The house wasn't nearly large enough for so many people and life was extremely uncomfortable for them all.

Mr Bucket was the only person in the family with a job. He worked in a toothpaste factory where he sat all day long at a bench and screwed the little caps on to the tops of the tubes of toothpaste after the tubes had been filled. But a toothpaste cap-screwer is never paid much, so there wasn't even enough money to buy proper food for them all. The only meals they could afford were bread and **margarine** for breakfast, boiled potatoes and cabbage for lunch, and cabbage soup for supper. AND the one thing that Charlie longed for more than anything was … CHOCOLATE.

Even worse, in the town where Charlie lived there was an ENORMOUS CHOCOLATE FACTORY. In fact, it was the largest and most famous in the world!

One day, it so happened that Willy Wonka, who owned the factory, announced that he would invite five lucky children who found Golden Tickets hidden underneath the wrapping in his chocolate bars to visit his factory. Not only that, but they would all receive a gift of sweets and chocolate to last a lifetime!

Well, of the five children who won, Augustus Gloop was one and, believe it or not, Charlie was another!

a Why is life difficult for Charlie?
b What does he eat for breakfast, lunch and dinner?
c What is special about the chocolate factory in his town?
d What is the special prize that Charlie wins with the Golden Ticket?

4.5 Read and respond

3 **Read and listen** to the next extract about what was inside the Chocolate Factory. Answer the questions.

The Chocolate Room

Mr Wonka opened the door. Five children and nine grown-ups pushed their ways in – and oh, what an amazing sight it was that now met their eyes!

They were looking down upon a lovely **valley**. There were **green meadows** on either side of the valley, and along the bottom of it there flowed a **great brown river**.

What is more, there was a **tremendous waterfall** halfway along the river – a [1]**steep** cliff over which the water curled and rolled in a solid sheet, and then went crashing down into a boiling **churning** whirlpool of **froth** and spray.

Below the waterfall (and this was the most astonishing site of all), a whole mass of enormous glass **pipes** were dangling down into the river from somewhere high up in the ceiling! They really were [2]**enormous**, those pipes. There must have been a dozen of them at least, and they were sucking up the brownish muddy water from the river and carrying it away to goodness knows where.

Graceful trees and bushes were growing along the riverbanks. In the meadows there were thousands of buttercups.

'There!' cried Mr Wonka, dancing up and down and pointing his gold-topped **cane** at the great brown river. 'It's all chocolate! Every drop of that river is hot melted chocolate of the [3]**finest** quality. The waterfall is the most important!' Mr Wonka went on. 'It mixes the chocolate! It churns it up! It pounds it and beats it! It makes it light and frothy! No other factory in the world mixes its chocolate by waterfall! And do you like my meadows? Do you like my grass and my **buttercups**? The grass you are standing on, my dear little ones, is made of a new [4]**kind of** soft, minty sugar that I've just invented! I call it swudge! Try a blade! Please do!'

a   Point to the words in **blue** in the pictures.
b   Find and match the **green** words to a word with a similar meaning.

| type | best | high | very big |

c   Find two verbs to describe what the waterfall does to the chocolate.
d   What is 'swudge'?

Glossary

margarine: similar to butter
valley: the land between two hills
froth: a mixture of bubbles and liquid
buttercup: a small yellow flower
cane: a stick to help you walk
churn: to mix something hard

4 Food

4 Read and listen to Augustus Gloop's accident and answer the questions.

Augustus Gloop's accident

Automatically, everybody bent down and picked one blade of grass – everybody, that is, except Augustus Gloop, who took a big handful of chocolate from the river.

When Mr Wonka turned around and saw what Augustus Gloop was doing, he cried out, 'Oh, no! Please, Augustus, please! I beg of you not to do that. My chocolate must be untouched by human hands!'

'Augustus!' called out Mrs Gloop. 'Didn't you hear what the man said? Come away from that river at once!'

'This stuff is fabulous!' said Augustus, taking not the slightest notice of his mother or Mr Wonka. 'Gosh, I need a bucket to drink it properly!'

'Augustus,' cried Mr Wonka, hopping up and down and waggling his stick in the air, 'you must come away. You are dirtying my chocolate!'

'Augustus!' cried Mrs Gloop.

'Augustus!' cried Mr Gloop.

But Augustus was deaf to everything except the call of his enormous stomach. He was now lying full length on the ground with his head far out over the river, lapping up the chocolate like a dog.

'Augustus!' shouted Mrs Gloop. 'You'll be giving that nasty cold of yours to about a million people all over the country!'

'Be careful, Augustus!' shouted Mr Gloop. 'You're leaning too far out!'

Mr Gloop was absolutely right. For suddenly there was a shriek, and then a splash, and into the river went Augustus Gloop, and in one second he had disappeared under the brown surface.

a Why is Mr Wonka angry with Augustus?
b What happens to Augustus?
c Where do you think Augustus goes?

5 Put the sentences in the correct order.
Now act out what happens in the story!

a Mr Wonka gets angry with Augustus and asks him to stop.
b But Augustus puts his hand in the chocolate river instead.
c Augustus falls into the river and disappears.
d Augustus doesn't listen. He lies down and eats the chocolate from the river.
e Everybody picks a blade of 'swudge' grass.

4.5 Read and respond

6 **Vocabulary:** Which adjective best describes Augustus?
   Which adjectives are positive and negative? Make two groups.

   > generous   helpful   greedy   selfish   mean   kind

7 **Talk:** Use the adjectives to talk about people you know.

   My sister is never selfish. She always shares her sweets with me.

8 Choose an adjective from Activity 6 to complete this description.
   Can you think of examples of this kind of behaviour?
   Which adjective is the opposite of the missing adjective?

   > If someone is ...., they like having things all for themselves and don't want to share with others. This feeling can make people do bad things, like Augustus in the story.

9 **Values:** Being generous
   Look at the examples of ways that we can be generous to each other.
   When have you been generous to someone else?
   When has someone been generous to you? Tell your partner!

   - Sharing things with each other
   - Helping each other with something difficult
   - Choosing a special gift
   - Making something special for someone

   I made a special cake for my granddad's birthday

   My brother always helps me with my homework, even if he's busy.

4 Food

4.6 Project challenge

Project A: Create a tasty treat!

Create a new kind of cake

1. Work in pairs. What types of cake can you see in the photos? Which is your favourite? What do you like about it?

2. Decide on what kind of cake you are going to make and who it is for.

3. Is it for a special occasion?

4. Find out what ingredients you need to make it, and make a list of them.

> Gingerbread man
> eggs
> flour
> sugar
> butter

5. Invent a name for your cake.

6. Write a short description about how to make it.

   Remember to use **connecting words** such as: **before**, **when**, **then** and **after that**.

   Use **cooking verbs** too: peel, prepare, mix.

7. Make your tasty treat at home with an adult. Take a photo of it or bring it into class. Display it along with your description.

4.6 Project challenge

Project B: Find out about where food comes from

1. Draw a picture of your favourite food or drink, or take a photo of the packaging.

2. Find out where your food comes from.
   - Is it produced or made in your town/city or country?
   - Does it come from a different country?
   - How was it grown or made?
   - How far has it travelled?
   - How was it transported?

3. Tell your partner about your food or drink.

   What food did your partner choose?
   Did you find out anything surprising?

> Remember to use sentences with **is/are + past participle** to describe a process:
>
> It is made from...
>
> It is mixed with...
>
> It is grown in...

Did you have any problems while you were doing your project?
How did you solve them?

4 Food

> 4.7 What do you know now?

What can we discover about food?

1 Write about what you had for lunch today or yesterday. Remember to use determiners:

some   any

2 Write sentences about the food in your fridge at home. Use these quantifiers:

a little   a few   a lot of   plenty of

3 Write (at least) four facts about how chocolate is made.

4 Can you remember how Rosa grew the cress plant in lesson 4.3? Tell your partner. Use these verbs to help you:

grow   clean   rinse   put   fold
press   cut

5 Think of adjectives to describe your favourite food or dish. Write sentences with these verbs:

look   taste   smell   feel

6 Think about the story in lesson 4.5. How did Charlie win his visit to the Chocolate Factory? Name two amazing things Charlie saw in the Chocolate Room.

Look what I can do!

Write or show examples in your notebook.

	😐	🙂
I can talk about what children in other countries eat for breakfast around the world.	○	○
I can explain how chocolate is made.	○	○
I can write about quantities of things.	○	○
I can describe how to grow cress using connecting words.	○	○
I can write a poem about a fruit.	○	○
I can understand a story with a food theme.	○	○

5 Adventures

We are going to...

- **talk about** what makes a good adventure story
- **use instructions** to draw a superhero
- **use** different words to describe personal qualities
- **create and act out a story** in the past tense
- **write** our own adventure stories
- **enjoy** an adventure story
- **create** an adventure project.

Getting started

What makes an adventure story?

a   What adventure stories do you know? What do you like or dislike about them?
b   How is an adventure story different from other stories?
c   What kind of places and characters make good adventure stories?

5 Adventures

> 5.1 Creating an adventure story

We are going to...
- talk about what makes a good adventure story.

1 **Talk:** Think of an adventure story that you like.
Draw three things from the story and show a partner.
Can your partner guess the story?

2 Look at the book covers.
What do you think the adventure stories are about?

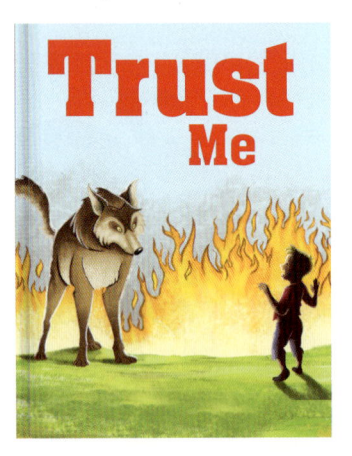

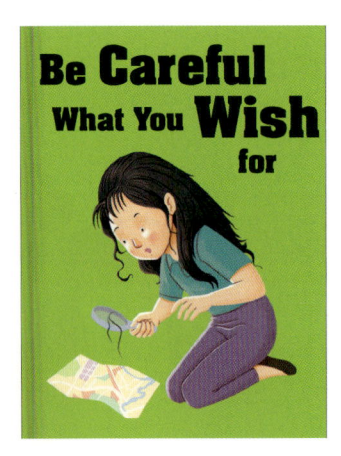

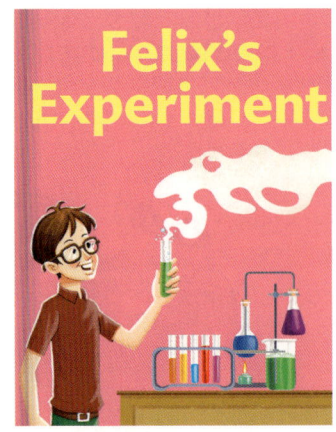

a **Trust Me**

b **Be Careful What You Wish for**

c **Felix's Experiment**

3 **Listen** to three story descriptions.
Match each story with a book cover from Activity 2.

4 **Vocabulary:** Match the parts of stories to the descriptions.

| characters | dilemma | title | setting |

a _____ : the name of the story

b _____ : the place or situation at the start of the story

c _____ : the people in the story

d _____ : a problem or difficult situation to be solved

5 Can you use the 'parts of a story' words to describe your pictures in Activity 1?

Listening tip

Use pictures

Use pictures and photos to help you understand what the listening text is about.

The title of my story is 'First Class Mystery' and it's set in a school. The characters names are...

5.1 Think about it

6 **Listen** to the first two story descriptions again.
Are the sentences **true** or **false**? Correct the false ones.

a   Leila wants to solve crimes like her father. **true / false**
b   One day Leila's father doesn't come home. **true / false**
c   When her father doesn't come home, Leila asks the police to look for him. **true / false**
d   Felix only does science experiments at school. **true / false**
e   He discovers something that can give him amazing powers. **true / false**

7 **Read** the sentences from story 3 and match to the story parts.

1	character(s)	a	Trust Me
2	setting	b	Kai, a 10-year-old boy
3	dilemma	c	It's the year 1414 and 10-year-old Kai is running for his life. His village is on fire and his family are lost.
4	title	d	Kai runs into the forest and is stopped by a beautiful wolf. The animal says she can help him find his family. But can Kai trust her or will he find himself in greater danger?

8 Which of the three adventure stories would you like to read? Why?

I like Be Careful What You Wish For because I like detective adventure stories.

9 Work in pairs. Describe an adventure story.

Brainstorm in pairs. Write down more adventure stories that you like. Think about adventures in books, comics and films.

Choose one story and write a short description using the story parts:

- character/s
- setting
- dilemma.

Don't write the name of the story title!

Read your description to another pair. Can they guess the film or book?

5 Adventures

> 5.2 Create a superhero

We are going to...
- use instructions to draw a superhero
- use different words to describe personal qualities.

1 **Talk:** In pairs, talk about your favourite superheroes or story characters. What special powers or skills do they have?

2 **Word study:** Match the personal quality adjectives to their descriptions.

1	brave	a	very strong
2	intelligent	b	very good at running and jumping
3	powerful	c	always a good friend
4	honest	d	not afraid of dangerous or difficult situations
5	loyal	e	very clever
6	athletic	f	always tells the truth

Key words: Drawing

create: make something new

guidelines: lines to help you draw

press: to push down on something

rub out: remove pencil marks with an eraser

add: to increase the number or amount

describe: say what something is like

3 Which adjectives describe your favourite superheroes or story characters? Describe a character to a partner but don't say the name. Can your partner guess who it is?

4 **Read and listen** to the text. When you **create** a superhero, what is the first thing you draw? What is the last thing you do?

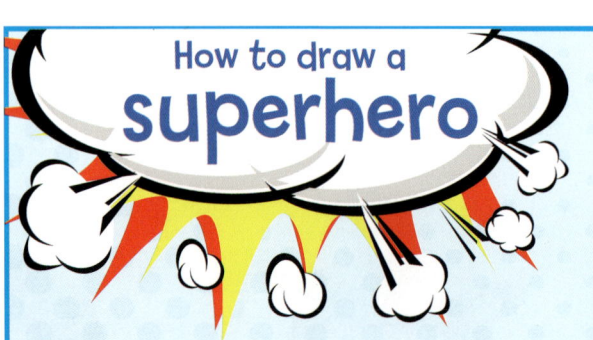

How to draw a superhero

- Draw your superhero's head.
- Draw a simple stick person with a circle for a head. These are your **guidelines**.
- Don't **press** too hard on your pencil.

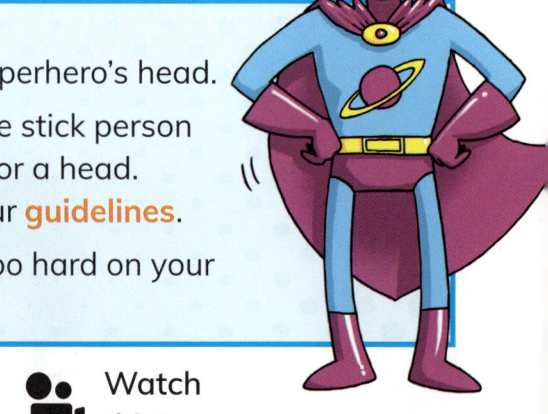

Watch this!

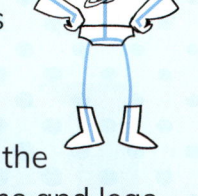

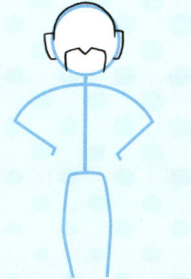

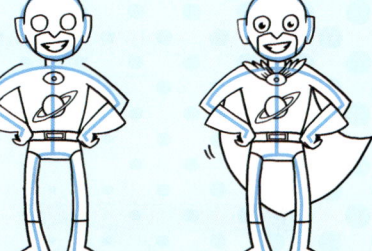

5.2 Art and design

- Use a light pencil line, then you can **rub out** the guidelines later.
- Decide now if your superhero is a boy or a girl. Is he/she wearing a mask? What is the expression on his/her face?
- Draw your superhero's body.
- **Add** the rest of your superhero's body. Use the guidelines to draw arms and legs.
- Think about your superhero's clothing. What is he/she wearing? Boots? Armbands? A cape? A belt?
  Does he/she have a special symbol or logo? Is he/she holding anything?
- Your cartoon superhero is complete! Rub out the guidelines and add some colour!

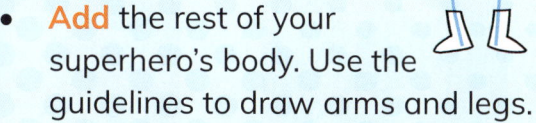

5 **Use of English:** Read the Language detective box and underline all the instruction words in the text.

   <u>Draw</u> your superhero's head.

6 Find five words to describe things a superhero wears.

7 Draw and talk about your own superhero.
   - Use the instructions to draw and colour your own superhero. Don't show your partner yet.
   - Give your partner instructions on how to draw your superhero. **Describe** his/her face, body and clothing. Give as many details as you can.

     Draw a mask like a cat. Draw some boots and a big belt.
     Colour the boots dark blue.
   - Compare your partner's picture with yours. How similar is it to your picture?

Language detective – Instructions

Draw a simple stick person.
Add some colour.
Don't press too hard on your pencil.

Start with the instruction word like this:
~~You~~ **Draw** a simple stick person.

5 Adventures

5.3 Telling a story

We are going to...

- create and act out a story in the past tense.

1 **Talk:** Think of a time when you had an adventure. When did it happen? Where were you?

2 Find the words in the pictures.

campsite   sniff   black bear   bush   hide   stare

a   b   c   d

3 **Read and listen** to the introduction. Match the description to one of the pictures.

> Last year I went on an adventure holiday with my family. We stayed at a campsite by a huge lake in the mountains. It was far away from any cities and there were lots of wild animals and birds. My dad said that a few black bears lived in the forest by the lake. Every day we looked for black bears. But we didn't see one…until…

4 Read and listen. Put the pictures (a–d) in order. Then read again to check.

> One evening, my big brother, Jack, and I were walking back to the campsite. It was getting dark. Then we saw it. A strange black shape on the road…
>
> 'Look Jack! What's that?' I said. The black shape moved towards us, getting bigger and bigger. Jack stopped, 'Tom, it's a bear! We need to hide and fast!' He pushed me towards a bush. 'Quick, get behind that bush!'
>
> We hid behind the bush and looked through the leaves. I could see the bear nearby. It stood high on its back legs and sniffed the air. 'Look, Jack,' I said, 'It's here. It's sniffing the air! It's enormous!' 'It can smell us!' Jack said, 'It's coming to get us…'

5.3 Talk about it

5 **Talk:** Why do you think the bear stopped and sniffed the air?
What do you think happened next?

6 **Listen** to the final part of Tom's story and check your predictions. What happened in the end?

7 **Use of English:** Read the introduction to Tom's story again and underline all the past simple verbs. Which verbs are *regular* and *irregular*?

8 Read and complete the final part of the story. Use the past simple verbs in the box. Then listen again to check.

> **Language detective – Past simple**
>
> We use the **past simple** to talk about actions that happened in the past, when we know **when** the actions happened.
>
> **Last year** I **went** on an adventure holiday with my family. We **stayed** at a campsite by a huge lake…
>
> Past simple verbs can be **regular** and **irregular**. Regular verbs end in **-ed**.

| was | ran | pulled | sniffed | ~~turned~~ | looked | stood |

The bear grunted loudly. It ¹<u>turned</u> to the bush. My heart was beating fast…Too scared to move, we stared at the bear. It ² _____ the air again. Time seemed to stand still!

Then slowly the bear turned and ³ _____ ahead. It ⁴ _____ over to the side of the road, to a big rubbish bin. It ⁵ _____ up again, pushed open the lid, put its enormous paw inside and grabbed a leftover hamburger with great enthusiasm.

The bear wasn't interested in us after all. The hamburger ⁶ _____ far more exciting!

'Take a photo!' I whispered. Jack ⁷ _____ his phone from his pocket. 'Otherwise no one will ever believe us!'

9 **Pronunciation:** Listen and repeat the lines from the story. Does the narrator sound bored, happy or afraid? How do you know? What happens to their voice?

10 **Talk:** In groups, practise retelling and acting out the story.

11 Present the story to the class. Add sound effects and read with expression!

> **Speaking tip**
>
> When you tell a story, read it with expression! This brings the story alive for the listener.

5 Adventures

> 5.4 Adventure stories

We are going to...

- write our own adventure stories.

1 **Read and listen:** What can you remember about Tom's story in lesson 5.3? Listen to the sound effects and put the sentences in the correct order for the story.

   a The bear stopped, stood up and sniffed the air. Did it know the boys were nearby? _____

   b The bear wasn't interested in Tom and Jack. It wanted the leftover hamburger from the rubbish bin! _____

   c One evening, Tom and Jack saw a bear coming towards them. They ran and hid behind a bush! _____

   d Last year Tom and his family stayed at a campsite by a lake. Every day they looked for black bears. _____

2 Match the sentences a–d in Activity 1 with a story part. Two sentences match one story part.

   1 The story setting
   2 Tom and Jack's problem
   3 The solution to the problem

3 **Word study:** Read the sentences in Activity 1 again. Find three time expressions that tell you *when* something happened. What other time expressions do you know?

4 **Write:** Look at the sentences and add the correct punctuation.

   a You did really well he said
   b Can you see that bear she asked
   c That's amazing he shouted
   d Be quiet she whispered

Writing tip

Punctuation for dialogue

'Look Jack**!** What's that**?**' I said**.**

'Look**,** Jack**,**' I said**.** 'It's here. It's sniffing the air**!**'

5.4 Write about it

> **Writing tip**
>
> **Make a story plan**
>
> When you write a story, make a plan first to organise your ideas.

5. Roll and write! Work in pairs and follow the instructions.
   Roll the dice four times to choose a time, a place, a character and a dilemma.

	Setting: time	Setting: place	Character	Dilemma
⚀	Last year	in an adventure playground	a scientist	got caught in a huge storm
⚁	Two weeks ago	half way up a mountain	a football team	got lost
⚂	One evening	on top of a skyscraper	a detective	did a crazy experiment
⚃	On a sunny morning	deep in the jungle	a twin brother and sister	found a strange car
⚄	Last weekend	in the middle of a football pitch	an astronaut	discovered a big bag of money
⚅	Last summer	high above the city in a helicopter	a school teacher	tried to invent a flying machine

6. **Write:** Use your ideas from Activity 5 to write your story.
   - Use the information from the chart to plan your story. Add more details. How do they solve the problem?
   - Use longer sentences to start the story and set the scene.
   - Use short sentences to describe the exciting bits!
   - Add dialogue.

5 Adventures

5.5 The Seekers

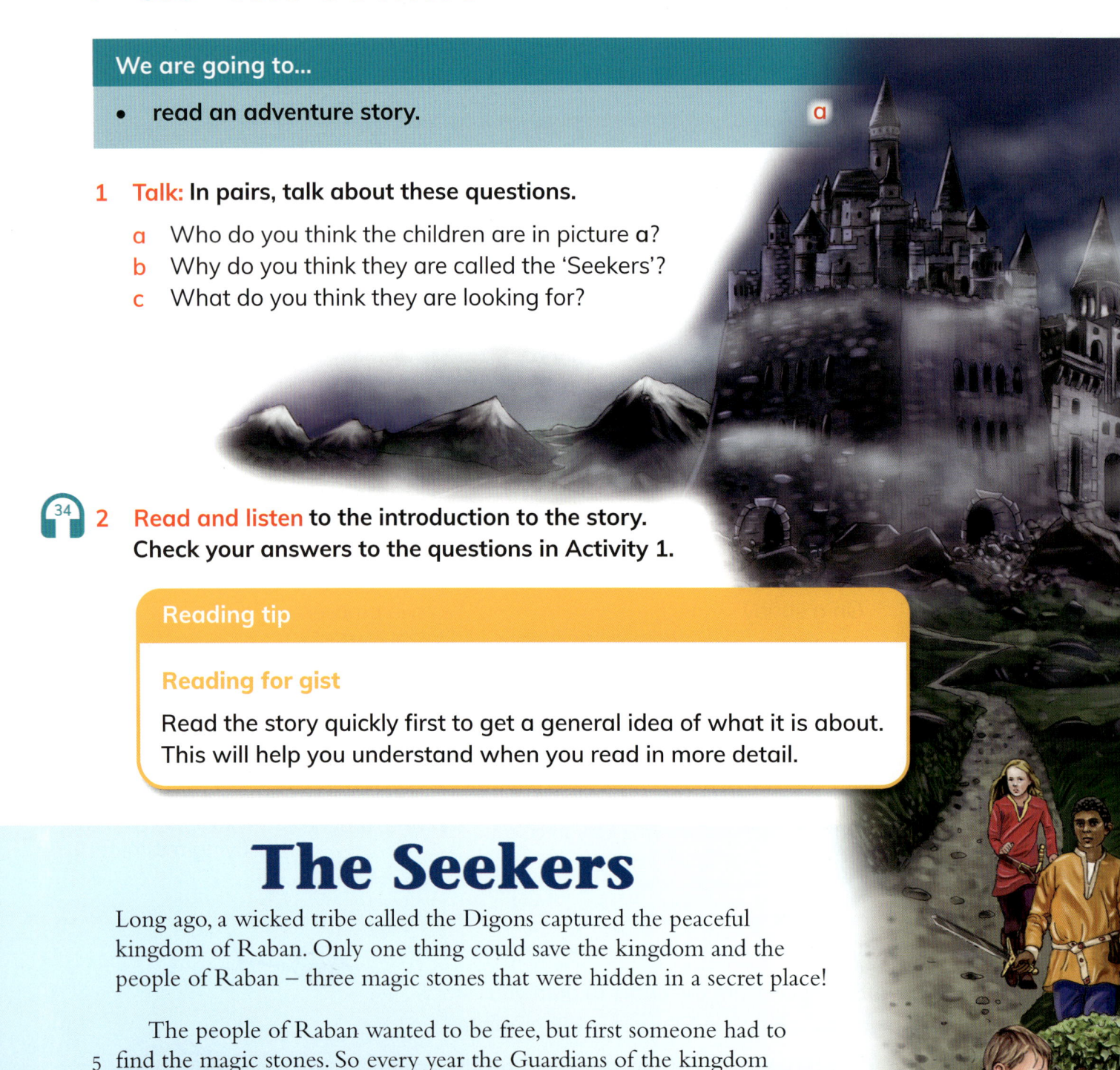

We are going to...
- read an adventure story.

1 **Talk:** In pairs, talk about these questions.
   a Who do you think the children are in picture **a**?
   b Why do you think they are called the 'Seekers'?
   c What do you think they are looking for?

2 **Read and listen** to the introduction to the story. Check your answers to the questions in Activity 1.

> **Reading tip**
>
> **Reading for gist**
>
> Read the story quickly first to get a general idea of what it is about. This will help you understand when you read in more detail.

The Seekers

Long ago, a wicked tribe called the Digons captured the peaceful kingdom of Raban. Only one thing could save the kingdom and the people of Raban – three magic stones that were hidden in a secret place!

The people of Raban wanted to be free, but first someone had to
5 find the magic stones. So every year the Guardians of the kingdom chose a special boy or girl to go on a journey to find the stones. Before the Guardians chose the special boy or girl, they gave them a test. They wanted a boy or girl who was brave, strong and intelligent. But the journey was very difficult and dangerous. So far, no one had finished the
10 journey and no one had found the stones.

5.5 Read and respond

Then one day, a young boy called Kehan came to do the test. He was a little boy with a big heart. He wanted to discover the secret place, find the stones and save the kingdom!

15 To his surprise, Kehan passed the test. The Guardians said that he could take two friends with him on the journey. He chose his good friend Bariel and another boy, Horaf, to go with him. The Guardians gave each child a sword. The swords
20 had magic powers to protect the children on their difficult and dangerous journey.

Now our three heroes are at the beginning of their journey in the wild countryside of Raban. In front of them are two paths. On the left, there
25 is a path through thick forest down to the valley. On the right, there is a narrow mountain track…

3 **Read and listen to the introduction again and answer the questions.**

- a What happened to the kingdom of Raban?
- b What was special about the stones?
- c Who do you think the Guardians were?
- d What did the Guardians do every year?
- e Who did Kehan choose to help him?

4 **Word study:** Look at the pictures b–g, which show the next part of the story in the wrong order.

- a Find these things in the pictures:

> a ravine   a sword   a flash of light   the beasts

- b What do you think happens next?

5 **Listen** to the next part of the story. Check your predictions and put the pictures b–g in the correct order. Which way did the children go at the beginning of their journey – left or right?

87

5 Adventures

6 Listen again and match the sentence halves. What do you think happened to the beasts?

1 Suddenly the children **heard**
2 They **saw** three beasts
3 The beasts **leapt**
4 The children **ran**
5 The magic swords **lifted** them

a into the air.
b towards the ravine.
c at the children.
d a terrible sound.
e in front of them.

7 Use of English: Find six examples of the past simple in the story.

Regular	Irregular
captured (capture)	gave (give)

8 Talk: What do you think happened next? What happened to the children? What happened to the beasts?

I think that the children...

Maybe the beasts...

5.5 Read and respond

9 **Vocabulary:** Which children in the story do these adjectives describe? Why?

> intelligent   honest   brave   loyal   athletic   powerful

I think Kehan is brave because…

10 **Values:** Being brave

What jobs are there where people do brave things?
Do you know anyone who does one of these jobs?

A firefighter is very brave because…

11 Read the sentences about being brave.
Which ones describe someone you know or have read about?

a   Someone who puts him/herself in danger to save someone else's life.
b   Someone who has a serious illness, but tries to be happy when other people are around.
c   Someone who does something that makes them feel nervous or scared, especially if it will help other people.
d   Someone who stands up for another person who is weaker.
e   Someone who has a disability, but still participates in activities with everyone else.
f   Someone who faces something difficult with a calm attitude.

12 **Talk:** Tell your partner about the sentences you have chosen.

Last week, I read a story about a boy who…

My aunt is very brave because…

5 Adventures

> 5.6 Project challenge

Project A: Create your own comic strip

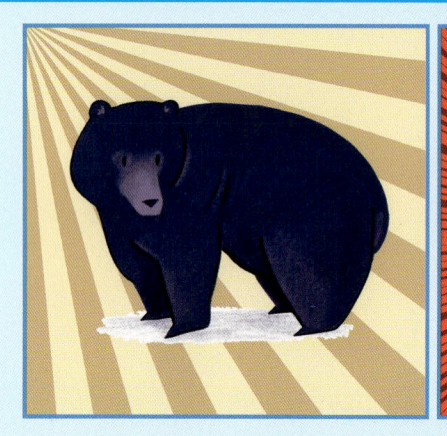

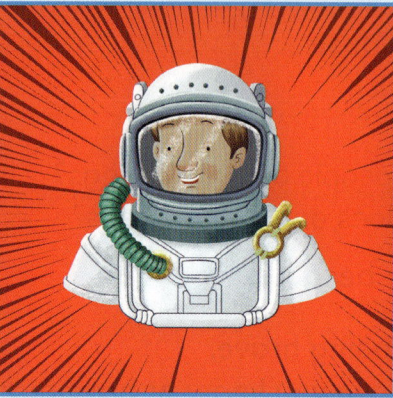

1. In pairs or in groups, brainstorm ideas for a comic strip. Use the 'Roll and write!' game in lesson 5.4 to help you think of your own ideas.
2. Plan your comic strip story using the story plan in lesson 5.4. Think of a title too.
3. Write your story in your notebooks. Use the past simple, adjectives and time expressions that you have learned in this unit.
4. Divide your story into 6–8 parts. What is the most important thing that happens in each part? Take 6–8 pieces of paper. Draw a picture to show the most important and the most exciting parts of the story.
5. Write the different parts of the story under the pictures. Add dialogue in speech bubbles next to the characters.
6. Stick the pictures and the story parts onto a big piece of card or poster paper. You have now created a storyboard!
7. Present your comic strip to your class.

5.6 Project challenge

Project B: Write the ending to *The Seekers* story

Work in a small group.

1. Read and listen to the story again. Compare your ideas for the next scene of the story. Decide together on the best idea for the story ending.

2. Use the story plan in lesson 5.4 to look at the different parts of the story and plan the rest of the story.

3. Work together to write the rest of the story in your notebooks. Use the past simple, adjectives and time expressions. Include dialogue and pay attention to punctuation.

4. Type up your story and decorate it with pictures.

5. Present your story ending to the rest of the class. What happens in the end? Do the Seekers find the stones? How?

6. As a class, vote on the most interesting and exciting ending for the story.

What materials did you use for your project?

5 Adventures

> 5.7 What do you know now?

What makes an adventure story?

1 Write five important instructions for drawing a superhero.

2 How many adjectives can you remember to describe personal qualities? Think of five synonyms and opposites for the adjectives (more if you can!).

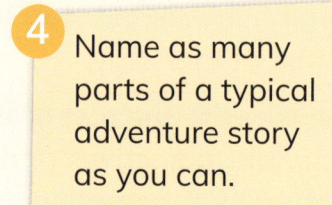

3 Think of five adjectives to describe a story character that you like. Make five sentences about them.

_____ **is intelligent because she….**

4 Name as many parts of a typical adventure story as you can.

Title,

5 Can you remember five irregular past simple verbs from The Seekers story? Write the past simple forms. Now make five sentences about the story using these verbs.

6 Think of an example of someone you know being brave. What brave thing did they do?

Look what I can do!

Write or show examples in your notebook.

I can understand a short adventure story.

I can draw and describe a superhero.

I can use different words to describe personal qualities.

I can act out a story and read aloud with expression.

I can write a short adventure story.

I can talk about brave actions.

I can create an adventure project.

6 > Going places

We are going to...

- **compare** ways of getting to school
- **find** out about road safety
- **use** prepositions of direction to practise giving directions
- **write** a description of a special journey
- **read** a short story
- **create** a project on a transport topic.

Getting started

How can we travel safely?

a Look at the pictures. How many ways of travelling can you see? What are the differences?

b What things can you see to help you travel safely? Which do you use?

c How many ways are there to travel around your town or city? Which do you think is the best way? Why?

Watch this!

6 Going places

> 6.1 Getting around

We are going to...
- compare ways of getting to school.

1   Test your knowledge of transport with this quick quiz!

   1   Which type of transport travels by air?
       a   a boat   b   a car   c   a helicopter
   2   Which type of transport doesn't need fuel?
       a   a bike   b   a motorbike   c   a plane
   3   What type of trains are **underground** or **metro** trains?
   4   Name one type of transport that uses electricity.
   5   If we walk to a place, we travel…
       a   by foot   b   on foot   c   in foot

2   **Talk:** Look at the photos. Which of these types of transport have you used? Where to? Which did you like best?

a   b    c 
d    e    f

3   **Vocabulary:** Find these types of transport in the photos in Activity 2.

| ferry | motorbike | tuk-tuk | tram | train | car |

6.1 Think about it

4   **Listen** to five children talking about how they get to school every day. Match the speakers to the photos.

5   Listen again. What are the good and bad points about each type of transport?

6   In pairs, talk about how you get to school. Describe one good and one bad point about your journey.

I cycle to school. I like it because…   *The only problem is that…*

7   **Read** the article quickly. How does Daisy get to school? How long does the journey take?

All over the world, children travel to school in different ways. Eleven-year-old Daisy lives in the remote village of Los Pinos in Columbia. Here, there are only two ways she can get to school – a two-hour **hike** through the jungle or a one-minute **zipwire** ride down the main road near her school. Every morning she takes the terrifying ride across the treetops, over a deep **canyon** and over a river. And she doesn't travel alone…she is the oldest child in her family and she has to help her two younger brothers get safely to the other side too. She fixes her brothers, one by one, into their **harnesses** and sends them down the **cable**. Then she follows them. She travels down the cable at a speed of nearly 50 kph.

Daisy makes the journey every day, but it never gets any easier. She says that she still gets nervous every time she rides over the treetops just to get to school.

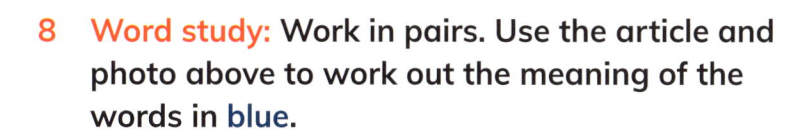

8   **Word study:** Work in pairs. Use the article and photo above to work out the meaning of the words in blue.

9   Read the article again and answer the questions.
   a   What other way could Daisy get to school? Why doesn't she?
   b   How does Daisy help her brothers?
   c   How fast does the zipwire travel?
   d   How does Daisy feel when she's travelling like this?

10   Find other phrases that use *get* in Activity 7.

11   **Talk:** Work in pairs. Can you think of safer ways for Daisy and her brothers to get to school?

Language focus – Uses of get

We **get** to school by tram
(get – travel)

She **gets** nervous every time…
(get – a change of feeling or situation)

Maybe they could cycle to school …

95

6 Going places

> 6.2 Road safety

We are going to...
- find out about road safety.

1   **Talk:** How do you usually travel? What can you do to travel safely by bike, car or on foot?

I usually travel by bike. I wear...

2   **Read and listen** to the text about road safety. Check your ideas from Activity 1.

1   Our school is on a main road in the town centre. It's really busy with lots of cars, lorries and buses. I ride my bike to school and I always wear a helmet.

2   In the winter here, it gets dark really early. When I walk home from school, I always wear reflective armbands so drivers can see me clearly.

3   I know that you **mustn't** go near big lorries, even if they are not moving. The drivers often can't see things behind them. That means they could reverse into you if you are standing too near.

4   You **should** always use pedestrian crossings to cross busy roads. Sometimes I can't find a pedestrian crossing so I find a quiet place to cross the road, away from corners and parked cars.

5   Our mum always tells us to wear seatbelts in the car, but my little brother hates wearing his seatbelt! Sometimes he tries to take it off, so my mum stops the car and makes him put it on again.

6.2 Health and safety

3   Read the text again and complete the table in your notebook.

What keeps you safe?	When?
a helmet	when you ride your bike

Key words: Giving advice

should – advice

mustn't – a rule or order

Language detective – Present simple

Routines/habits: I **ride** my bike to school and I always **wear** a helmet.

States: In the winter here, it **gets** dark really early.

Some present simple verbs are **irregular**, for example **be** and **have**.

4   **Use of English:** Complete the sentences with the verbs below.
    Use the Language detective to help you. Then tick the sentences that are true for you.

   wear   ride   travel   not be

   a   There _____ a pedestrian crossing on my street.
   b   When it's dark, my dad always _____ reflective armbands.
   c   My sister often _____ a bike and she always wears a helmet.
   d   When we _____ in the car, we always wear seatbelts.

5   **Talk:** These three signs help to keep people safe when they are walking, cycling or driving. What do you think the signs mean?

   a   b    c

6   What are the dangers on the roads near to your home and school?
    Design a sign to warn people about the dangers.

   • Brainstorm ideas for your sign. Is it about a danger on the road?
     Is it a sign to warn adults or children about dangerous behaviour?
   • Choose one idea to make into a sign.
   • Present your sign to your class. Explain what the sign is and why
     your neighbourhood needs this sign.

6 Going places

> 6.3 Getting around cities

We are going to...
- design town maps to practise giving directions.

1 **Talk:** Do you live in a town or a city? What are the five best places to visit? How do you get there?

I think the best place to visit is the...

2 **Vocabulary:** Which of these places did you talk about in Activity 1?

> picnic site   swimming pool   beach   theatre   sports centre
> cinema   playground   hotel   museum   restaurant   theme park   park

3 Put the places from Activity 2 into these categories. Can you add any more to each list?

Sports and activities	Entertainment	Eating	Sleeping

4 **Listen:** The Diaz family are in London for the day. Listen to Dad's conversation in the tourist office.

a Which types of transport are mentioned?
b Which place from Activity 2 is mentioned?

Listening tip

Predicting answers

When you are completing notes, try to guess the missing words before you listen.

5 **Read** Dad's notes. Try to guess the missing words and then listen again to check your answers.

> The Natural History ¹_____ – wonderful wildlife ²_____.
> Underground – South Kensington.
> From here ³_____ to the museum (about five minutes).
> Go out of the office – turn ⁴_____ and walk across the road.
> Turn ⁵_____ after the theatre – walk up that street.
> The entrance to the underground is ⁶_____ the right.

98

6.3 Talk about it

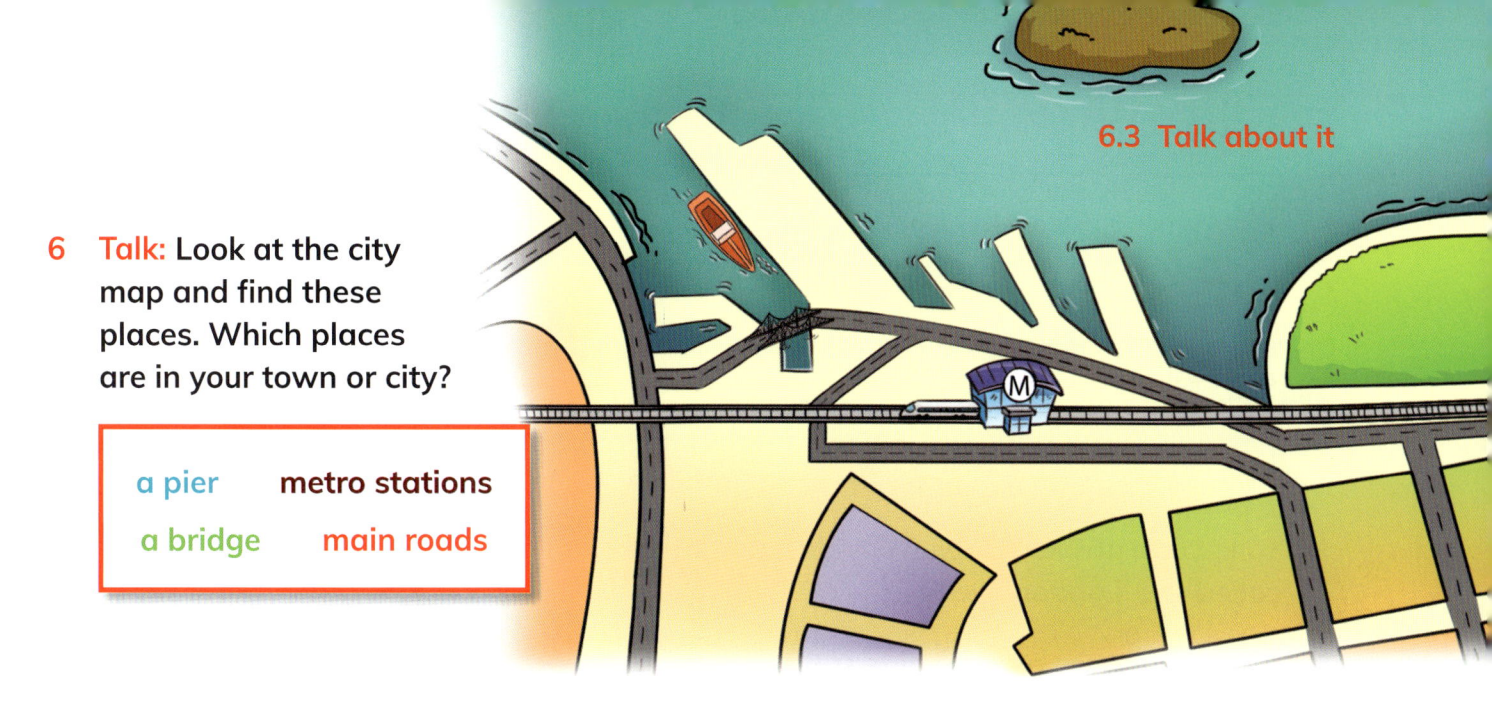

6 **Talk:** Look at the city map and find these places. Which places are in your town or city?

- a pier
- metro stations
- a bridge
- main roads

7 Match each map symbol to a place in Activity 2.

a   b   c   d

8 Work in pairs to design a town map.

  a   Choose **six** places from the word box in Activity 2.
      Design map symbols for the places.
  b   Design your own town by putting symbols in the boxes on the map.
      Think about the best places to put different types of buildings.
      Which places could be near to a pier? On a main road? By the water?
  c   You can also use the symbols in Activity 7 and repeat the same place more than once. You can also design a symbol for a place that is not mentioned in this lesson.

> **Language detective – Prepositions of direction**
>
> **From** here you can...   Walk **across/up** the road/street...
>
> **Go** out of the door...   Walk **towards** the Post Office/pier
>
> **On** the left/right   The entrance **to** the Underground/bus stop ...

9 **Use of English:** Choose a place on your map and don't tell your partner. Give your partner directions. Can they find the correct place on your map?

> Start at metro station 1... walk towards the...then turn right...

6 Going places

> 6.4 Travel experiences

We are going to...
- write a description of a special journey.

1 **Talk:** Look at the photos. Why do you think it is called the 'London Eye'?

2 Close your eyes and imagine travelling on the London Eye. Talk to your partner and write five things you might see.

3 **Read** Mia's description of her experience on the London Eye.

We climbed into the glass capsule. It had huge windows from floor to ceiling. We stood at the windows and the capsule started to rise slowly. My little sister giggled and pointed. I stared at the river, then we went up, up into the clouds. I felt excited and nervous at the same time! We climbed higher and higher over London. I could see amazing buildings: palaces, famous places, towers and domes and glass skyscrapers that sparkled in the sun. All colours, shapes and sizes. I could see bridges, parks and a thousand streets with tiny cars and people. From up there, they looked like little insects going backwards and forwards.

We climbed slowly, higher and higher, under the enormous blue sky. Then we came down to earth. In our 30-minute journey, I had travelled over the whole city of London!

Past simple tense
Interesting verbs
Powerful adjectives

---

4 **Word study:** Match the descriptive words in Mia's description to the words below. Which words are verbs and which are adjectives?

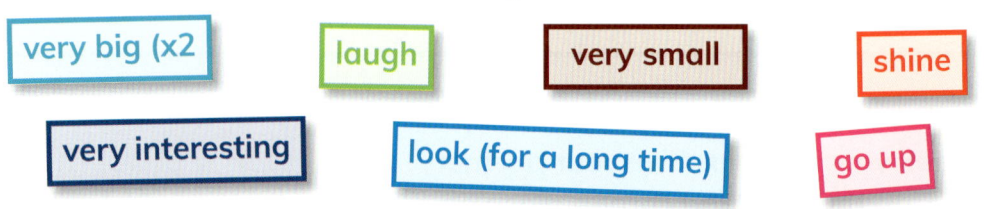

- very big (x2)
- laugh
- very small
- shine
- very interesting
- look (for a long time)
- go up

5 Why do you think Mia uses the descriptive words and not the words in Activity 5?

6.4 Write about it

6   **Write:** Make the underlined phrases more interesting. Use the words and phrases in Activities 4 and 5 to help you.

   a   We were on the 60th floor of a <u>very tall building</u>.
   b   I <u>looked</u> out of the <u>windows</u>.
       The view was <u>very nice</u> – I could see <u>lots of places</u> below.

7   Put the sentences from Activity 6 together to make a paragraph. Add another sentence to describe what you could *hear or feel*.

8   **Talk:** Have you ever been on a special journey? Why was it special? Tell your partner.

   Your journey could be:
   - to see a special place or person
   - traveling on a special type of transport

9   **Write** a description of your special journey. Use the mind map, Mia's description in Activity 3 and the steps below to help you.

> **Writing tip**
>
> Like as a preposition
>
> We can use **like** as a preposition to describe and compare things.
>
> **They looked like little insects …**

My special journey

What did you do first?
What could you see?
Then what did you do?
What could you hear?
What did you do next?
How did you feel?

We climbed into the glass capsule.
It had huge windows from floor to ceiling.
We stood at the windows…
My little sister giggled and pointed.
I stared at the river…
I felt excited and nervous!

- Use your senses (**see**, **hear**, **feel**, **smell**) to help you describe your journey.
- Think of size, colours and shapes.
- Use strong words and powerful sentences, and use like for describing and comparing.
- You can use **like** for describing and comparing.
- Use the past simple tense.

10   **Present, display or publish your work.**

6 Going places

6.5 Lost in the Desert

We are going to...
- read a short story.

1 **Talk:** Have you ever got lost somewhere away from home? What did you do to find your way home?

2 Before you read, look at the pictures. How do you think this girl gets lost in the desert?

3 **Read and listen** to the story. Check your predictions and answer the questions after each part.

Lost in the Desert

by Margo Fallis

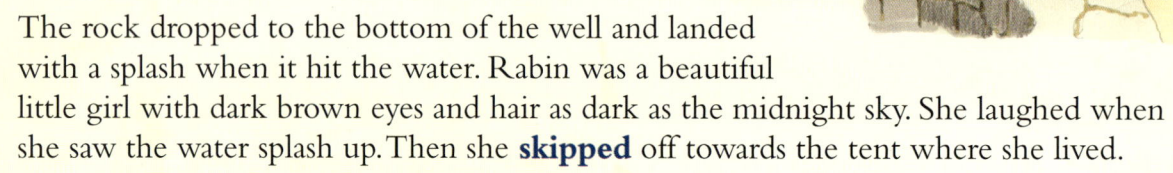

The rock dropped to the bottom of the well and landed with a splash when it hit the water. Rabin was a beautiful little girl with dark brown eyes and hair as dark as the midnight sky. She laughed when she saw the water splash up. Then she **skipped** off towards the tent where she lived.

5   Summer in the Egyptian desert could be very, very hot. Rabin's tent was in a small village in the arid desert, southwest of Cairo. Not many people ever came to the village to visit, but now and then a camel train would pass through. A tree sprouted up now and then from the parched earth.

a Where did Rabin live?
b What kind of home did she live in?

Sometimes she'd ask her friends, Karim and Yasmine,
10 to play with her. One day, they were walking along a sandy trail when they came to an area of trees. Rabin saw something moving off the side of the path. It was a furry rabbit. She wanted to follow it, but her mother had warned her never to leave the path; it was
15 dangerous. She'd told Rabin that she might get hurt or lost. Sometimes there were wild animals waiting in the bushes. But Rabin wanted to catch that rabbit.

102

6.5 Read and respond

She **ran** off the trail, following the rabbit through rocks and sandy soil. Karim and Yasmine tried to call her back, but she wouldn't listen. The rabbit hopped over a dead tree,
20 so Rabin followed it. It ran up a small hill. It **leapt** over a wide riverbed. While Rabin was running after it, the rabbit **jumped** into some thorny bushes and she lost sight of it.

c   What did Rabin want to do?

d   Did Karim and Yasmine go with her?

e   Did Rabin catch the rabbit?

She sat down in the shade of a tree and looked around at the unfamiliar surroundings. In the tree above hung a rather large beehive. As Rabin sat there, unaware of the hive, she noticed a lot of bees gathering around her. They were buzzing back and forth.
25 Rabin didn't like bees. She jumped up and ran as fast as she could.

She ran into the bushes and realised that she was lost. Nothing looked familiar to her. Where were Karim and Yasmine? Why hadn't she listened to what her mother
30 had said? She sat down on a rock and started to cry.

f   What happened when Rabin sat down to rest?

g   What did she do?

As she sobbed, she heard a hissing sound. She looked at the ground and saw a cobra. It was coiled up and its tongue was flickering in and out of its mouth. Its head was flat and wobbled back and forth. Rabin jumped up on top of the rock and watched the snake. It slithered across the sand, but then it slunk away. Now she really began to cry. She was
35 very frightened.

She **hopped** off the rock and started running back to the riverbed. She was walking along when she saw something move. Her heart jumped as she thought it was the rabbit. Maybe, if she followed it again, it would lead her back to Yasmine and Karim. She ran over to it, but saw it was a small fox, reddish brown with a bushy tail. It scurried off into the bushes.

h   What did Rabin see next?

i   How did she feel?

j   What did she do?

40 She hung her head down and **plodded** along. She noticed tracks by the riverbed, like a crocodile's. She couldn't see a crocodile, but she thought that one might be waiting nearby. So she ran quickly down the riverbed.

6 Going places

Now Rabin felt tired, hungry and afraid. The sun was setting below the horizon. The sky glowed a beautiful orange and red colour, but she didn't want to be alone in the dark.
45 She sat down in the sand, too tired to move. She lay her head on her hands and fell asleep.

> k How did she feel now?
> l What time of day was it?
> m What did she do?

When she woke up, the rabbit was standing by her head. Its little black nose was wet and rubbing against her cheek. Rabin stood up slowly. The rabbit didn't **run away**. It wanted Rabin to follow it.

50 She walked slowly and followed the rabbit back down the riverbed, past the crocodile tracks, past the rock where the cobra had slithered and past the tree filled with angry bees. The rabbit suddenly stopped. Rabin listened.

55 'Rabin. Where are you?' It was her father.

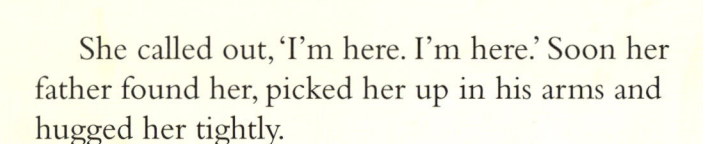

She called out, 'I'm here. I'm here.' Soon her father found her, picked her up in his arms and hugged her tightly.

60 'Where were you, Rabin? We've been worried about you. Yasmine and Karim told us you'd wandered off the path. You know you aren't supposed to do that,' her father scolded.

'I know, Father. I am very sorry. I'll never leave the
65 path again.' She turned and looked for the rabbit. Where did it go? She saw it running off into the trees. She smiled, took her father's hand then walked back home.

> n How did Rabin find her way home?
> o How did her father feel?
> p What did Rabin do?

6.5 Read and respond

> **Language detective – Past continuous: interrupted actions**
>
> She **was walking** along when she **saw** something move.
>
> (continuous action)   (short action)

4   **Use of English:** Look at the Language detective and match these sentences from the story. Check your answers in the text.

1 They were walking along a sandy trail	a when she saw something move.
2 While Rabin was running after it,	b when they came to an area of trees.
3 She was walking along,	c the rabbit was standing by her.
4 When she woke up,	d the rabbit jumped into some thorny bushes.

5   **Word study:** Find the verbs of movement in blue in the story. Work out the meanings or check your dictionary.

   a   Which one is the odd one out?
   b   Now compare the other verbs. Act out the verbs! How are the movements different?

6   **Listen** to the end sounds of the verbs from the story and put in the correct column.

/t/	/d/	/id/
dropped	raised	landed

7   **Values: Taking advice**

   a   What advice did Rabin's mother and father give her?
   b   What happened when she didn't listen to them?
   c   How did she feel?
   d   What did Rabin say to her father at the end?

8   **In pairs, ask and answer questions.**

   a   What advice do your parents or family members give you?
   b   Have you ever ignored their advice? What happened?

6 Going places

6.6 Project challenge

Project A: Design your own safety poster

1. **Brainstorm: What can you do to keep safe when you are not at home?**

   Think about:
   - What to do to prevent getting lost.
   - What to do if you get lost.
   - What to do to keep safe in the street.

2. **In pairs, prepare a poster to give advice to other children. What do other children need to know about keeping safe? Write 6–8 statements. Use the present simple to describe good safety habits and routines.**

   When you go out, always tell someone where you are going.

   > **Tip**
   >
   > **Sharing the task**
   >
   > Either write all the statements together; or take two or three statements each and work on your own. Then compare and check your sentences together.

3. **Check your statements together.
   Do they make sense?
   Are the grammar and spelling correct?**

4. **Make a poster with your statements. Decorate it: find pictures online or in magazines or draw your own. Make sure your handwriting is clear. Then display your poster on the wall.**

5. **Read your classmates' posters. Is there any advice that is different to yours?**

6.6 Project challenge

Project B: Plan a visit to your town or city for two visitors

Plan a visit

1. Two friends are coming to visit from another town.
   In small groups, brainstorm places to visit in your town or city.
   Which places do you think your visitors would like to visit?

2. Choose three places for them to visit on Day 1:
   - Say why you have chosen these places.
   - Describe how they can get there by different types of transport and by walking.

     They can get a bus to _____ then walk up the street and turn left at the…

   - Where would they go first?

3. Make a poster to show the places to visit and stay. Use photos to present your ideas to another group or your class. Divide the presentation up so that each person presents a small part.

4. Listen to your classmates' presentations.
   Which plan is the most interesting or fun for the visitors? Have a class vote!

> First, our friends can visit the…. There, they can…. They can get there by….

Did you find out anything surprising when doing your project?

6 Going places

> 6.7 What do you know now?

How can we travel safely?

1. Name **three** ways of getting to school. Give one good and one bad point about each one.

2. Write **five** sentences giving advice about road safety.

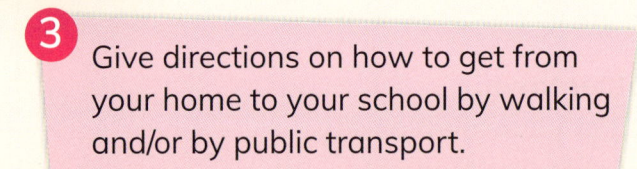

3. Give directions on how to get from your home to your school by walking and/or by public transport.

4. Write **four** sentences about your favourite type of transport. Say why you like it.

   I like travelling by train because…

5. Write **three** things that happened while you were travelling to school today.

   I like travelling by train because…

6. Which **three** sounds come at the end of **regular** verbs in the **past simple**?

7. What are the best pieces of advice your family or teacher has ever given you? Tell your partner.

Look what I can do!

Write or show examples in your notebook.

	😐	🙂
I can talk about how I get to school.	○	○
I can understand issues about road safety.	○	○
I can design a road safety sign.	○	○
I can give directions using a street map.	○	○
I can write a description of a special journey.	○	○
I can understand a short story.	○	○
I can pronounce the three sounds at the end of regular past simple verbs.	○	○
I can talk about the importance of taking advice.	○	○

Check your progress 2

1 **Read the clues and solve the crossword.**
Then put the words into the unit topics: 4 Food; 5 Adventures; 6 Going places

Across →

2 Sugar tastes like this
5 Very interesting or surprising
8 Very, very tasty!
10 A person in a story

Down ↓

1 Good at sports, especially running
3 A long yellow fruit
4 A place where you can play and climb things
6 This protects your head
7 When you don't want anyone to find you
9 Plants grow from these tiny things

2 **Find six words from Units 4, 5 and 6 and make a revision crossword to test your friends!**

Check your progress 2

3 Work in pairs. Play a game to correct the sentences!

Choose 0 or X. Roll a dice: highest number starts. Choose a sentence (1–9), correct it and put your 0 or X in the box. First person to get three in a line wins!

1 There isn't some bread.	2 There is a few milk in the fridge.	3 Not press too hard on your pencil.
4 Draws a simple stick person.	5 Go in of the door and turn right.	6 I ride my bike when it started to rain.
7 The shop is in the left.	8 There are any tomatoes.	9 Now adds some colour.

4 Imagine you are going to have a celebration. Which food would you choose?
You have three minutes to draw the food in your notebook. (Don't show your friends!)

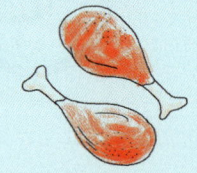

5 Your partner will listen, draw what you describe and ask questions too. Then compare your drawings.

> There's a little chicken and plenty of watermelon…

> Is there any chocolate?

6 In pairs, play 'word tennis' with the verbs below. When you say a verb from your line (A or B), your partner says the past simple form.

Student A: see   go   run   look   be   have   say   stay

Student B: live   do   make   try   give   want   can   finish

> see

> saw

7 Write four sentences about you in the past simple using the verbs in Activity 6. Make some true and some false. Then swap and guess which of your partner's sentences are true or false.

> Last year I went in a helicopter.

> I think that's false!

7 Australia

We are going to...

- **talk** about extreme weather around the world
- **discover** amazing facts about Australia
- **give** a presentation about a special animal
- **talk** about future plans
- **write** a blog post about our weekend
- **enjoy** a traditional story.

Getting started

What can we learn about one country?

a Look at the photos. What are they pictures of?
b How does this country look different to your own?

Watch this!

111

7 Australia

> 7.1 Weather around the world

We are going to...
- talk about extreme weather around the world.

1. Work in pairs. Write down all the adjectives you can think of to describe the weather.

2. **Talk:** Choose the phrases that describe the weather in your country at different times of the year.

3. Imagine you are talking to someone from another country. Describe the weather in your country at different times of the year.

Watch this!

It's stormy, with thunder and lightning.

It's sunny and mild.

It's hot and humid.

It's hot and dry.

It's cold and rainy.

It's snowy and frosty.

It's usually hot and humid from April to October.

4. **Vocabulary:** Match the words to the pictures.

a cyclone   a tornado   a blizzard   a flood   a drought

a   b   c   d   e

112

7.1 Think about it

5 **Listen** to the weather report. What type of extreme weather is happening? In which country and where?

6 **Vocabulary:** Match the adjectives and nouns to make collocations. Some of the adjectives match more than one noun.

blustery wind

Adjectives		Nouns
blustery	cutting	wind
thundery	strong	sky
turbulent	fierce	waves
crashing		sea

7 **Listen again** and check your answers to Activity 6.

8 Use the adjectives from Activity 6 to complete the sentences from the weather report.

a We have _____ skies today and a _____ wind is howling.

b The sea is _____ and I can see waves crashing onto the shore.

c Weather experts report that this _____ storm could become a tropical cyclone in a short time.

d I can hardly stand up because of the _____ and _____ wind.

9 **Talk:** What is the worst weather you have ever seen in your country? What happened?

10 When this type of weather happens, what safety advice would you give?

> When there is a tropical cyclone, you mustn't go out on the streets.

> Last year/summer, there was a flood …

7 Australia

> 7.2 Australia

We are going to...
- **discover amazing facts about Australia.**

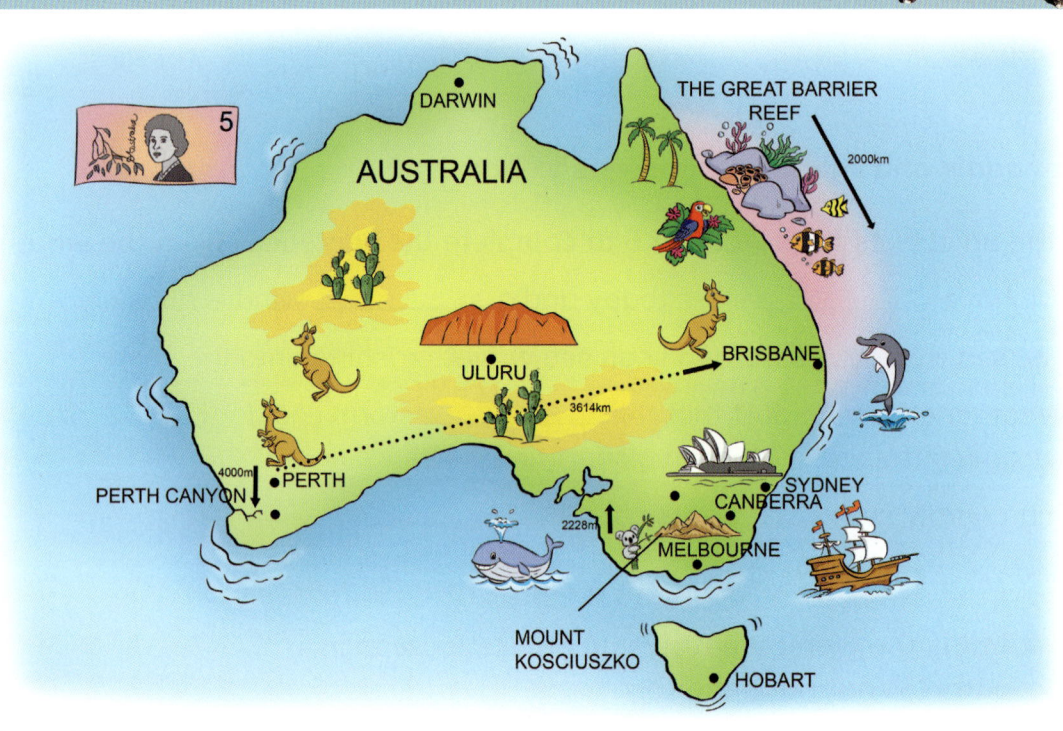

1   **Talk** in pairs.

   a   Is Australia a big country?
   b   Who lives there and what languages do they speak?
   c   Which animals and marine life live there?
   d   Does it have any special geographical features?

2   **Word study:** Find examples of the geographical features below on the map.

   desert   mountain range   coral reef   rock formation   coast   tropical rainforest

3   **Read and listen** to the fact file about Australia on page 115. Can you find the answers to the questions in Activity 1?

Reading tip

Noticing numbers

When you are reading, notice any numbers and figures. These will often help you to understand important information in the text.

7.2 Geography

Fact file: Australia

Facts and figures
The population of Australia is 25 million. There are many different types of people and religions, and nearly one quarter of Australians were born in other countries. The Aboriginal people are the only people who are native to the country.

Australia is the sixth largest country in the world and the main language is English. It has a land mass of nearly 7.7 million square kilometres. It is both a country and a continent. The currency is the Australian dollar, which is divided into 100 cents.

Geography
Australia has a varied landscape. Almost 20 per cent of Australia is desert. There it is hot and dry with hardly any rainfall. There are mountain ranges across the whole of the east coast, where the temperatures are sometimes below zero. There are also tropical rainforests in the north, where it's hot and humid. The amazing Great Barrier Reef is the world's largest coral reef and stretches for 2,000 km along the north-east coast. The total **length** of the Australian coastline is 35,877 km, which is very long! The **width** of Australia is impressive too. It takes five hours to fly from Brisbane to Perth, which is 3,614 km. If you drove for eight hours a day, it would take 5.5 days to do the same journey.

In the centre of Australia is the beautiful Uluru (known as Ayer's Rock outside Australia), a huge, mysterious sandstone rock formation that looks like it changes colour at different times of the day. It's an important place for the Aboriginal people of the area. The highest peak is Mount Kosciuszko in New South Wales, which reaches a **height** of 2,228 m. The Perth Canyon, which attracts exotic marine life and blue whales, can be found on the east coast, with a **depth** of 4,000 m.

Key words: Geography

length: the measurement of something from end to end
width: the distance across something from one side to the other
height: the distance from the top to the bottom of something
depth: the distance down from the top of something to the bottom

---

4 Find these numbers in the fact file. What do they refer to?

| 25,000,000 | 6th | 7,700,000 square metres | 1/5 |

5 List three types of natural environments that are mentioned in the fact file.

6 Find two similarities and two differences between Australia and your country. Use the fact file and the words in Activity 2 to help you.

7 Australia

> 7.3 Animal matters

We are going to...
- give a presentation about a special animal.

1 **Talk** in pairs.

   a   Which animals live in the wild in your country? Make a list with your partner.
   b   Write a **C** beside the common animals. Write an **R** beside the rare animals.
   c   Why do you think the animals you have marked with an **R** are rare?
   d   What is an endangered animal? Are any of your rare animals endangered?

2 **Look at the pictures and talk about the questions.**

   a   Have you ever heard of the animals below?
   b   What type of habitat do they live in?
   c   What do you think is special about them? (A clue: It's in their names!)

a laughing kookaburra

a lung fish

a dinosaur ant

3 **Listen:** Laura is giving a presentation in class about one of these special animals. Which one of them is she describing?

7.3 Talk about it

4 Listen to Laura again and complete the chart in your notebook.

Name	Curious fact	Country	Characteristics	Diet	Endangered Species (Yes/No)	Reasons
Dinosaur ant						

5 **Pronunciation:** Listen, repeat and practise the short form of *have*.

6 **Use of English:** Complete the sentences using the present perfect.

a Laura _____ (watch) a lot of TV programmes about Australian animals.

b They _____ (die) because of climate change and bushfires.

c Bushfires _____ (destroy) their habitat and homes.

d I have never _____ (hear) of the lungfish before.

e Have you ever _____ (do) a project about wild animals?

> **Language detective –**
> **Present perfect (indefinite time)**
>
> We use the present perfect when we are talking about our experience up to the present time.
>
> We make the present perfect with have / has + past participle.
>
> I **have been** to Australia.
> I **have never** seen a dinosaur ant.

7 Do a presentation about the kookaburra, the lung fish or a special animal from your country.

- Find information about your animal and complete the chart in Activity 4 in your notebook.
- Write out your presentation with the help of your teacher.
- Try to include a sentence using the present perfect.
- Practise reading your presentation out loud.
- Draw or find a picture of your animal, insect, fish or bird to show the class.

7 Australia

> 7.4 Taking a trip

We are going to...
- talk about future plans
- write a blog post.

1 **Talk** in pairs talk about why you would take a trip away from home. How can you keep in touch with people when you are away?

2 **Read** Jack's blog. What do you think is the main purpose of this trip?
   a To go snorkelling in the sea
   b To find out why fish and turtles are dying
   c To go on a boat trip.

Day 1 I'm sitting in my tent. We're camping tonight in the outback. I'm feeling scared because there are dangerous snakes and spiders out there! We set off from Darwin at 7 o'clock this morning and we've been at the campsite for three hours now. We ate our dinner under the stars and it tasted **amazing**! Tomorrow we're travelling to the beach so my mum can do her work. We're having a picnic there too!

Adjectives

Day 4 It's night-time now and I'm writing this by torchlight. This morning Dad and I went **snorkelling** for the third time in the sea. It has been fantastic every time! **We've seen lots of different fish** and we've seen two **turtles** since Tuesday! My mum says turtles are an endangered species in this part of Australia. She's working on a conservation project to find out why turtles and fish are dying.

Events that happened (present perfect)

Conservation projects help to keep wildlife safe and free to live in the wild. My mum collects bits of **rubbish** from the beach and sea. She tests them to see if they contain poisons that can kill the turtles. Her work is very important! I would like to be a conservationist too when I'm older.

Can't wait for tomorrow! **In the morning, Dad and I are going out on a boat trip** and then we're helping Mum collect rubbish from the beach.

Plans for the next day (present continuous)

3 What does Jack say about the words in blue in the text?

118

7.4 Write about it

4 Look at Day 1 and answer these questions.
   a How is Jack feeling as he writes his blog? Why?
   b What did he do earlier in the day?
   c What are they planning to do tomorrow?

5 **Use of English:** Find more examples of the present continuous with future meaning in Jack's blog.

6 Make notes on what Jack and his family did on their trip. Write them in the correct order.

> Day 1: set off from Darwin at 7am, arrived at the campsite
> Day 4:

Language detective – Present continuous with future meaning

We can use the present continuous to talk about actions or plans in the near future.

Tomorrow, **we're having** a picnic on the beach.

Writing tip

Making notes

When you make notes, you only have to write the key words not full sentences.

7 **Write** a blog post about your weekend.

Step 1: Planning	Saturday activities and Sunday plans Imagine it's Saturday evening. Make notes about… • things you have done up to now. • what you are doing now as you write. (Where are you? Where are you sitting?). • your plans for tomorrow (Sunday).
Step 2: Writing	Remember to use your plan and use the present perfect to talk about the things you have done and the present continuous for future plans. Include interesting information about what you can see and feel.
Step 3: Read and respond	Swap with 4–5 classmates. • Who did similar things to you? • Who has similar plans to you for Sunday?

8 Display or publish your work on the class or school blog.

7 Australia

7.5 Why the Emu Can't Fly

We are going to...

- read a traditional Aboriginal Australian story.

1 **Talk:** What traditional stories do you know from your country? Which one is your favourite? Do you know anything about animals? Do you know what an emu is?

2 **Read and listen** to the story *Why the Emu Can't Fly*. Who are the main two characters?

My favourite story is...

3 Read each part of the story and answer the questions at the end of each section.

Why the Emu Can't Fly

A traditional story from the Aboriginal people of Australia.

Dinewan the Emu was big and strong with **huge** wings that carried him over great distances. His wife had lots of children each year and he was well-respected and feared. Like all powerful
5 ones, he also had some enemies, especially Goomblegubbon the Brush Turkey.

He was jealous of Emu's power of flight and the way he could run **swiftly** over the vast plains without tiring. So he made a plan to hurt Emu, and he told no one about it except for his wife. He waited until he knew that Emu was going out on the plain to feed and he made
10 sure that he got there before him. He held his wings close by his body, ruffled up his feathers and sat on the ground where the grass was rich and long.

When Emu had eaten a lot of grass and was in a good mood, Brush Turkey spoke to him. 'Hello, I want to tell you something that I think you should know. The other animals are wondering why a big, strong bird like you chooses to fly everywhere, instead of walking.'

15 Emu looked at him with great surprise. How else could he get anywhere, he wondered. Brush Turkey continued, 'No one else would dare to tell you these things, Emu, but walking really is best. Flying is something that any bird can do; it's common and ordinary. It's only men and strong birds like you and me who can get about by walking. It's a sign that you are a special bird.'

7.5 Read and respond

20   Emu thought about it and replied, 'Hmm, perhaps you are right, I will have to talk about it with my wife this evening.' And off Emu went, **striding** across the plain to test Brush Turkey's words. His long legs carried him swiftly home to his wife.

    a   Why do you think the Brush Turkey wanted to hurt Emu?
    b   Why is walking better than flying according to Brush Turkey?
    c   How did Emu get home after listening to Brush Turkey?

    The next day, the two birds met again. 'I have thought about it and decided that you were right,' Emu said. 'My wife and I took off our wings last night. We were sad to lose them, but my
25 leg muscles are growing stronger already. I'll **race** you to that bush!'
Brush Turkey laughed and laughed. 'I can't believe that it was so easy to trick you with that **tale**, Emu. Your brains must be as small as a baby bird's. But if you want to, I'll race you.'

    Emu **sprinted** across the sun-baked ground. Brush Turkey waited until Emu had nearly reached the bush, then he **flapped** noisily through the air, **landing** well ahead of Emu.
30 'Ha, ha, what a fool you are, Emu,' he cried. 'The other animals will never respect a bird who cannot fly.' Emu was angry. He **rushed at** Brush Turkey, **striking out** at him with his powerful legs, but Brush Turkey just flew away laughing. Emu sadly walked home to tell his wife how he had been tricked.

    d   What did Emu and his wife do after listening to Brush Turkey?
    e   Who won the race?
    f   What was Emu's reaction?
    g   How did Brush Turkey respond?

A whole year went by. Emu never said anything to Brush Turkey about the loss of his
wings, and this **puzzled** Brush Turkey. Emu's legs grew stronger and soon he was able to run as fast as the other could fly.

One morning, Emu took his two largest children out with him, leaving his other fourteen in their mother's care. He met up with Brush Turkey and his wife and their noisy family. 'Busy?' asked Emu. 'Busy!' exclaimed Brush Turkey, 'It's hard work all day long just trying to keep all of the children's stomachs full and they still look so thin. We're trying to teach them to hunt for their own food, but we haven't had much luck so far.' 'Yes, I can see that,' replied Emu, 'But the trouble is that there are too many of them. They don't get a chance to grow big. We sent most of ours to live with other families. We thought that the only way to have strong, healthy chicks was to only keep the biggest. See how much bigger my two are than yours. The next generation will be real birds.'

Brush Turkey and his wife walked around the Emu's chicks and thoughtfully whispered together. Emu walked off with his chicks, chuckling quietly to himself.

The following day he met Brush Turkey on the plain. 'I have taken your advice, Emu,' Brush Turkey said. 'Here are my two biggest chicks. The others have gone to live with their aunts and uncles. What do you think of this strong pair?' Emu laughed and laughed. 'What a fool you are,' he said. 'A bird's strength lies not in his ability to use his wings, but in the number of his children. I am sorry for you, my friend, but perhaps it will teach you that brush turkeys are even more **foolish** than emus.'

And that is why emus have so many chicks but cannot fly, and why brush turkeys only lay two eggs each year.

h   When Emu and Brush Turkey met again, what problem did Brush Turkey have?
i   What solution did Emu suggest?
j   What did Brush Turkey do to his family?
k   What was Emu's reaction?

7.5 Read and respond

4 **Talk** in pairs. What do you think was the true reason that made Emu lose his wings?

    a   Brush Turkey wanted to have a smaller family.
    b   Brush Turkey was jealous of Emu and wanted to hurt him.
    c   Emu thought walking was better than flying.

5 **Do you think there is a message in the story? What do you think it is?**

6 **Word study:** Match the synonyms below to the words in blue in the story.

quickly	confused	very big	silly	story	hitting

7 Match the words in green in the story with the definitions.

    a   when birds move their wings very quickly
    b   try to run faster than someone in a competition
    c   walk quickly taking big steps
    d   run fast over a short distance
    e   move quickly towards someone
    f   touch the ground after flying in the air

8 **Values: What to do if you feel jealous**

    a   Have you ever felt jealous of someone? Why?
    b   What do you think is the best advice to take if you feel jealous of someone? Why?
- Try to be better than them.
- Try to hurt them.
- Think about the good things in your own life and focus on those things.

7 Australia

> 7.6 Project challenge

Project A: Make an endangered species 'flip-up' class poster

1. In groups, find out and make a list of the endangered species in your country and around the world.
   Choose a species you would like to find out more about.

2. Find out the following information on the internet, in magazines or in books about your chosen species. Make notes.

Name	Curious fact	Country	Characteristics	Diet	Why endangered
Bengal tiger	No two tigers have the same stripes	India	Strong and powerful	Deer and buffalo	Loss of habitat

3. Draw a picture of your animal and write a short paragraph about your endangered species. Use your notes and these key sentence starters to help you.

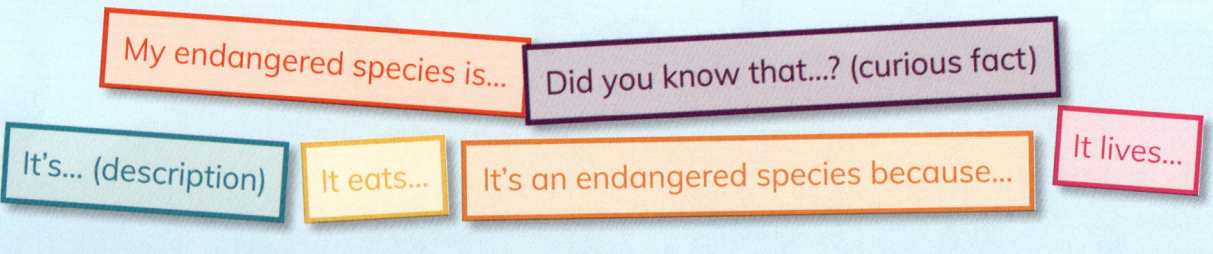

   - My endangered species is…
   - Did you know that…? (curious fact)
   - It's… (description)
   - It eats…
   - It's an endangered species because…
   - It lives…

4. Display your work on the flip-up poster.

7.6 Project challenge

Project B: Be international weather reporters!

1. In groups, choose a country to give a weather report on.
2. Your group will give a weather report at the beginning of your class, comparing the weather in your own country and your chosen country.
3. First, follow these simple steps to make a weather chart. Divide up the tasks in groups.

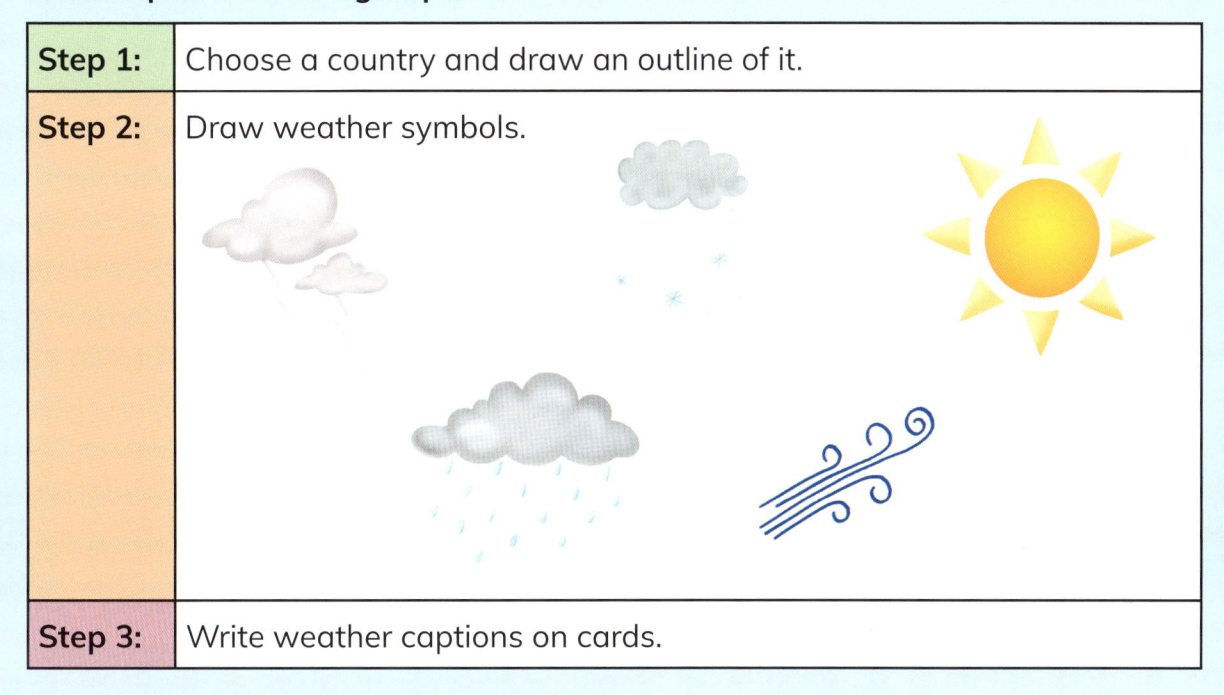

Step 1:	Choose a country and draw an outline of it.
Step 2:	Draw weather symbols.
Step 3:	Write weather captions on cards.

4. Check the weather online for your chosen country and give your weather report using a weather chart.

The weather today in Australia is......

10^0 Cold and rainy

5. Do a weather report for your own country and your chosen country to the class. Compare the weather for each one.

How well did your group work together on your project?

7 Australia

> 7.7 What do you know now?

What can we learn about one country?

1 Name four examples of extreme weather.

2 All of these adjectives except one can be used to describe the wind. Which is the odd one out?

- blustery
- fierce
- thundery
- cutting
- violent

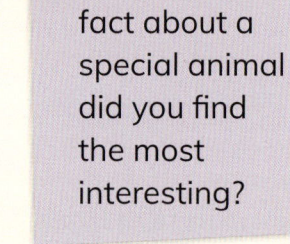

3 Name one fact about Australia for each of these categories:
  a general fact   b geography
  c climate

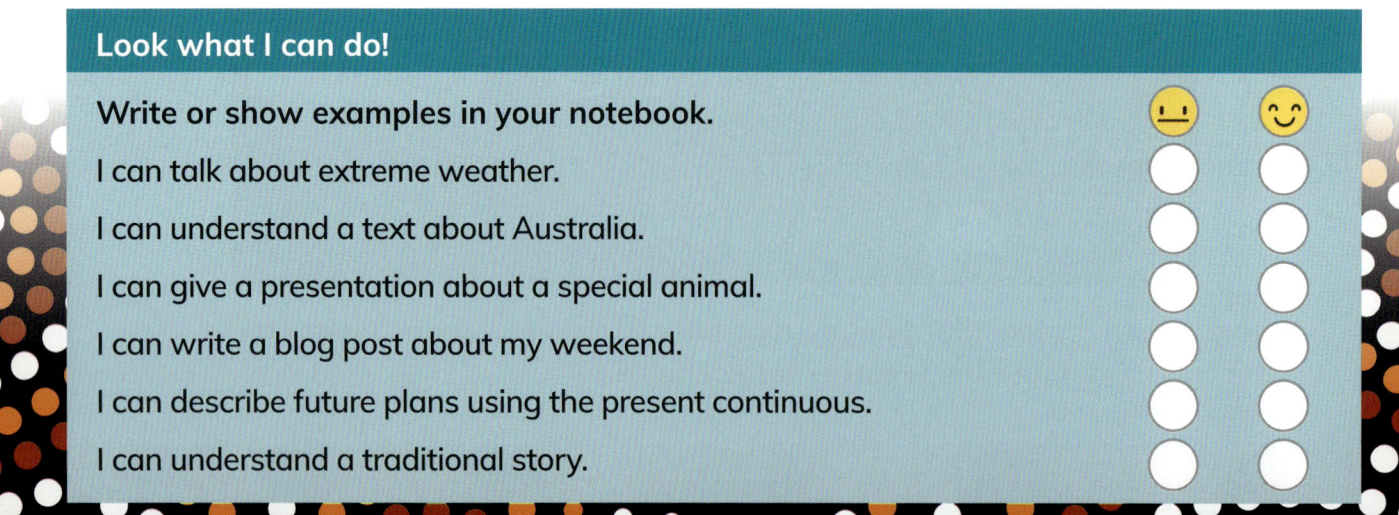

4 Give two reasons why animals become endangered.

5 What curious fact about a special animal did you find the most interesting?

6 Think about Jack's blog. What did his mum do on the trip? Why?

7 Give two examples of how Emu and Brush Turkey tricked each other in the story *Why the Emu Can't Fly*.

Look what I can do!

Write or show examples in your notebook.

I can talk about extreme weather.

I can understand a text about Australia.

I can give a presentation about a special animal.

I can write a blog post about my weekend.

I can describe future plans using the present continuous.

I can understand a traditional story.

8 Nature matters

We are going to...

- **find out about** environmental problems affecting our Earth
- **explore** how we can change our habits
- **make** promises about our environmental habits using **will**
- **write** a personal recount about a local natural habitat
- **understand** and enjoy a short story about the future
- **choose** and **create** a project about recycling.

Getting started

What's happening to our Earth and what can we do to make a difference?

a   What is the difference between these two photos?
b   What is happening?
c   How does it make you feel?

Watch this!

8 Nature matters

8.1 Nature alert!

We are going to...

- find out about the problems our Earth is facing.

1 **Talk:** These artworks illustrate some of the problems facing our Earth.
In pairs, talk about what you think they are trying to tell us.

2 **Vocabulary:** Match the environmental problems to the art.

> air pollution   rising sea levels
> plastic pollution   melting ice caps

🎧 46 3 **Listen** and match the descriptions to the art in Activity 1.

a

Melting world

b

Support

c

Open the curtain

d

Plastic whale

128

8.1 Think about it

4 **Use of English:** Match the sentence halves.

1 **Pollution** is something…
2 **Rubbish** is something…
3 The **environment** is the natural world…
4 **Global warming** is a term…
5 **Eco-friendly** is a product…
6 An **environmentalist** is a person…

a that/which we don't have use for anymore.
b that/which is dangerous for our health and the Earth.
c that/which we live in.
d that/which respects the environment.
e that/who cares for and looks after our natural world.
f that/which describes how the Earth is getting hotter.

Language detective – Defining relative clauses

Who and **that** give extra information about a person.

An **environmentalist** is someone **who** looks after our natural world.

Which and **that** give extra information about an object, place or thing.

Air pollution is something **that** is dangerous for our health.

5 Look at the photo. What do you think this text is about? Read and complete with *who*, *that* or *which*.

The turtle's lunch

One day, the giant sea turtle was swimming in the sea looking for its lunch. It saw something ¹_____ was white floating in the water. It looked like a jellyfish, ²_____ was its favourite food. 'Yummy,' thought the turtle, ³_____ was swimming towards its prey. It opened its mouth and took a bite of the jellyfish, but it was a piece of white floating plastic, ⁴_____ made the turtle very sick. It was washed ashore and a person ⁵_____ was walking along the beach helped save its life.

6 How can you stop plastic from getting into the sea?

8 Nature matters

> 8.2 Protecting our planet

We are going to...
- explore how we can change our habits.

1 **Talk:** In pairs, look at these things. What are they made of? Which ones do you use a lot? When you've used them, what do you do with them?

   a   b   c   d

2 **Read and listen** to the text and think about your answers to the questions in Activity 1. Which of your habits do you need to change?

Our plastic oceans

Plastic history
Plastic is a strong material made by people. It has all kinds of uses and can be made into almost any shape. It is used to make airbags, bicycle helmets and medical products. All of these can save people's lives.

Plastic problems
But plastic is not **biodegradable**. Nearly every piece of plastic EVER made still exists today. Scientists think that 8.8 million tonnes of plastic waste goes into our seas every year! Plastic rubbish often blows into rivers, which then flow into the oceans. Over time the sea breaks the plastic into smaller parts called **microparticles**, which can hurt or kill marine life.

Plastic solutions
If we don't change our plastic habits, scientists think that by 2050 there will be more plastic in the oceans than fish! One million single-use plastic bottles are bought every minute around the world, so we need to **reduce** their use and replace them with bottles we can **reuse**. We need to use cloth bags instead of plastic bags to carry our shopping in, and our governments need to build better facilities to **recycle** this material.

8.2 Environment

> **Key words: The environment**
>
> **biodegradable:** a material that can turn back into elements found in nature
> **microparticle:** a very small part of something
> **reduce:** to use less of something
> **reuse:** to use something again
> **recycle:** to process something so it can be used again

3   Read the text again and answer these questions.
   a   Find an adjective that describes plastic.
   b   Why can plastic save people's lives?
   c   Why is there so much plastic in our oceans?
   d   What does the sea do to plastic over time?
   e   What can we do to reduce and reuse plastic objects?

4   Find facts in the text that match these numbers.

   8.8 million tonnes   1 million   2050

5   **Write:** Work in pairs. Write three sentences using *have to* about the environment. Use ideas from the text and give reasons for your answers.

   We **have to** stop using plastic water bottles **because** they are dangerous to marine life.

6   Write three things you have learned from the text, two things which are interesting and one question you have.

7   Work in groups. Find out about ways to recycle plastic to make something new.
   Find interesting ideas, then present your findings to the class. Vote on the most exciting idea!

> **Language focus**
>
> **Re** – when we add **re** at the start of a verb, it often means to do the action again.
>
> I **re**wrote my story to correct the spelling.
> We should **re**use plastic bags.
>
> Find more examples of your own. Use a dictionary.

> **Language focus**
>
> **have to**
>
> We use **have to** to express obligation.
>
> We have to reduce our use of plastic straws because they are dangerous for marine life.

8 Nature matters

> 8.3 Rethinking our world

We are going to...

- Make promises about our environmental habits using *will*.

🎧 **1** **Listen** to two children doing a class survey about how eco-friendly they are. Tick the pictures that illustrate Dani's answers.

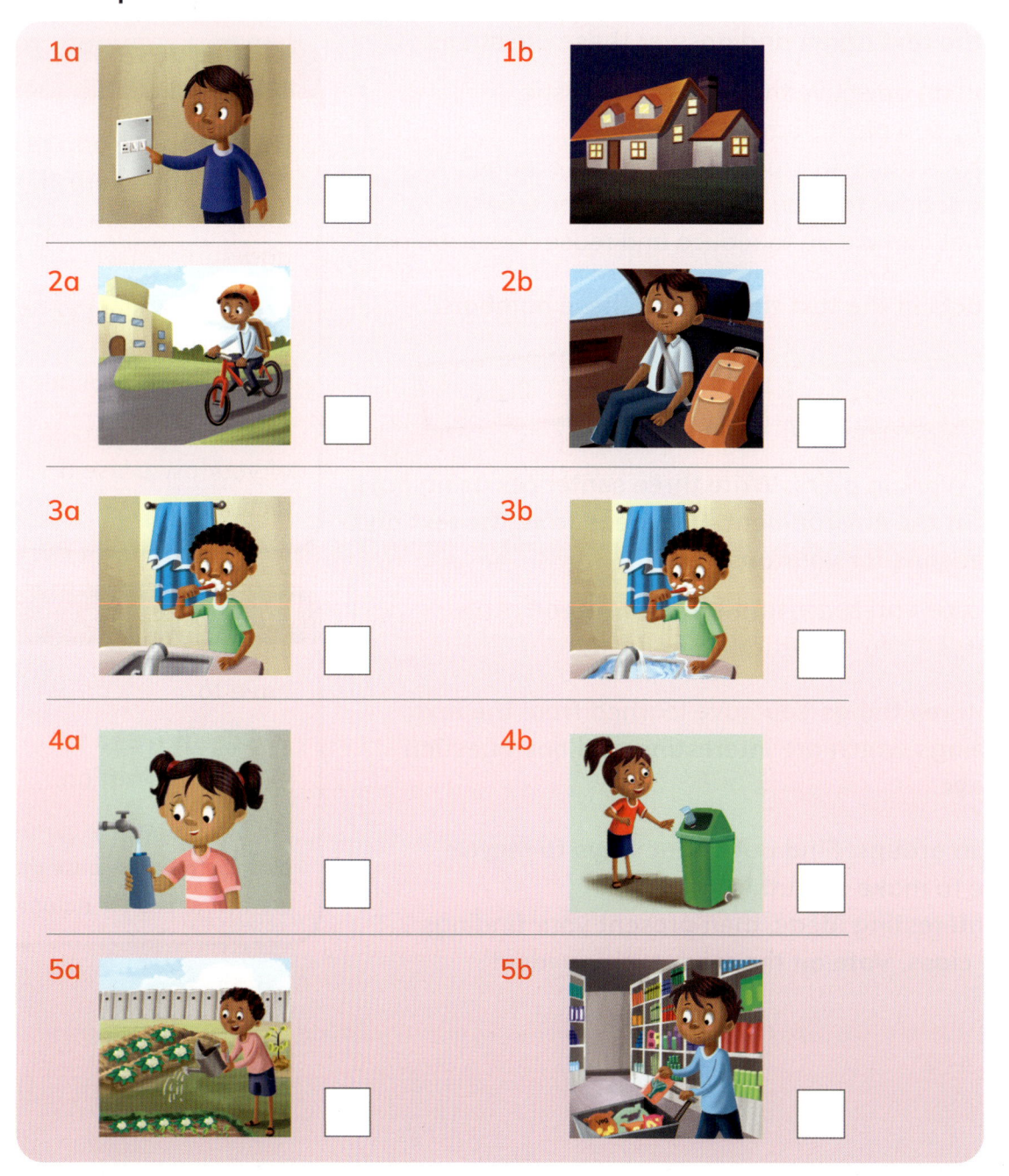

1a 1b

2a 2b

3a 3b

4a 4b

5a 5b

8.3 Talk about it

2 **Read** the quiz summary. How green is Dani?

As: If you have mostly As then you are very green! You are a number one planet protector! Keep up the good work!

As and Bs: If you have a mix of As and Bs then you are quite green! You do care for the environment, but you need to do more. Set yourself more eco-challenges!

Bs: If you have mainly Bs then you're not very green. You've got a lot of work to do! Remember our Earth needs looking after by you too! Take some of the ideas from this unit and put them into practice!

3 Match the phrases to the pictures in Activity 1.

a save water __3a__
b turn off lights _____
c grow vegetables and herbs _____
d ride your bike _____
e use single-use plastic bottles _____
f waste water _____
g buy food in plastic packaging _____
h leave the lights on _____
i use a car _____
j use reusable water bottles _____

4 **Do a survey.** Write five more questions. Ask three classmates your questions.

1 Do you **turn off the lights** when you are not in a room? Yes/No

5 Read the quiz summary again. How green are your friends?

6 **Listen:** Dani talks about how he will be more eco-friendly in the future. What Earth promises does he make?

7 **Pronunciation:** Listen and repeat and practise the contracted form of **will**.

8 **Use of English:** Think about your answers to the quiz. Do you need to change any of your habits? Write some Earth promises that you will start tomorrow and present them to your class.

> **Language detective – Will for promises**
>
> We use **will** to talk about our promises for the future.
>
> I promise I**'ll help** my mum more in the vegetable garden.
>
> I promise I**'ll ride** my bike more.

133

8 Nature matters

8.4 A personal recount

We are going to...
- write about a visit to a local park, river or coastline.

1 **Talk:** What can you see in this picture? Where are the children going? What do you think the children are doing? Tell your partner.

2 **Read** the description. Were your predictions correct?

OUR VISIT TO THE LOCAL RIVER

[In class we were learning about the environment, and about how our habits and the waste we create affects nature. Miss Smith wanted us to do a project about nature and rubbish in our community, so she arranged a trip to our local river to see if it as 'clean' and 'green'.] *(Paragraphs)* *(First person pronoun)*

It was a beautiful day and **I** was excited about going for a walk along the river with my classmates. We arrived at school at the usual time on Tuesday morning and then waited for a bus to take us all to the river. **The trip only took about 15 minutes**. *(Fact)*

When we arrived, Miss Smith gave out clipboards with a worksheet for us to do. Our task was to write down the names of any wildlife we saw and to fill in a chart about the rubbish we found too.

The first thing we saw was a group of tiny ducklings swimming behind their mother. **They were so cute**! We saw a frog near the riverbank, croaking among the reeds and even a shoal of small fish. *(Opinion)*

(Past tense) **But I was shocked** at the amount of rubbish I could see on the riverbanks. There were plastic bottles, bags and cans. It was horrible to see so much rubbish in this lovely place. So, we've decided to go back at the weekend to clean up the rubbish.

8.4 Write about it

3   Read the description and find the answers to these questions.

   a   What was the purpose of their trip?
   b   How did the child feel about going on this visit?
   c   Did they see any wildlife there?
   d   How did they record the information they found?
   e   How did the writer feel about the rubbish?

4   **Use of English:** When is the past simple in a personal description? Find examples of regular and irregular verbs in the text.

5   Read the examples from the text and label (F) for fact or (O) for opinion.

   a   The teacher arranged a trip to the local river.
   b   They were so cute!
   c   The trip only took about 15 minutes.
   d   I was shocked at the amount of rubbish I could see.

6   **Write** a personal recount about an exciting or memorable school trip you have been on.
    Write about your experiences and feelings.

Writing tip

Facts and opinions

Look for words like **I think** and **I was**, which give an opinion, and figures and statements that are true for facts.

Step 1: Make notes	• The school trip you want to write about. • Where did you go and why? • How did you travel there? • How did you feel about going on the visit? • What was your task (if any)? • What did you see and do? • Did you enjoy the trip?
Step 2: Organise your recount	• Use paragraphs to organise the information. • Write things in the order that they happened. • Write in **past tenses**. • Use first person pronouns **I** and **we**. • Include facts and your opinions.
Step 3: Read, compare and check	Swap with a partner. Check for spelling and grammar mistakes!

8 Nature matters

> 8.5 The Future of the Present

We are going to...
- read a short story about the future of our environment.

1 **Talk:** In pairs, look at all the pictures. What do you think the story is going to be about?

🎧 51 2 **Read and listen** to the story. Check your ideas.

The Future of the Present
by Malini Venkataraman

It was a sunny afternoon. Pinky and Chotu were bored. They had watched enough television and had finished their homework too. Just then, Chotu remembered his remote control car he bought
5   years ago. He quickly ran to the storage room and looked for his car. Pinky followed him. As they were looking for the car, Pinky found a dusty, rusty old thing that looked like the remote of Chotu's car.

'Chotu! Look what I've found!'

10   'It doesn't look like my car's remote control. Wait, what are these strange buttons?'

'Let's take it to Dad and show him,' said Pinky.

'I wonder what will happen if I press this?' said Chotu.

'Don't!' shouted Pinky warily. Too late! Chotu pressed the button with his finger.

3 **Answer the questions.**

a   What did the children want to do when they finished their homework?
b   What did the remote look like?
c   What do you think will happen now after Chotu pressed the button?

8.5 Read and respond

They both felt dizzy. The only thing they saw now was black and green. Their heads whirled. Rubbing their eyes, they were surprised to see their new surroundings. They were new to them because they were in a completely new place!

They saw a big steel castle with strange machines sticking out of it. They both stood in front of three massive doors. They were red, green and blue.

Pinky and Chotu chose to enter through the blue door, which opened into a vast, deserted land. The place was empty. There were no people and there were hardly any trees. There were only some tall, thorny bushes.

'How terrible!' Chotu said to Pinky. 'There's no greenery here at all! What is this place? Where have we come to?'

4 What adjectives does the writer use to describe this place?

big   steel

5 **Word study:** Find words in the story that mean:
    a   very big
    b   different or odd
    c   an area with just land
    d   sharp parts of plants
    e   no one or nothing inside
    f   trees, bushes and grass

137

8 Nature matters

When Pinky turned her head, she saw a huge shadow cast over them.

'A …a…a! M-O-N-S-T-E-R!" shouted Chotu. They were scared so they started to run.

35 They tried to run away but they got tired. They stood helplessly in front of the monster. They looked closely at it. It was made of junk and electronic waste. It smelt horrible!

'Please don't do anything to us,' begged Pinky.

'Ha, ha, ha!' laughed the monster loudly. 'I am the garbage monster! And you
40 humans created me. You threw all your waste on the Earth, you cut down trees and made mountains of electronic waste. You created a concrete jungle and you created me!'

Neither of the children could say a word. They felt very ashamed.

'Yes,' said Chotu. 'We are sorry for our behaviour. We realise now the effect of our actions and irresponsibility.

45 Please let us go and we will see that everyone will now take care of the environment because the health of the Earth is our future, and nature matters!'

A strong wind started to blow and pulled them back to their room. 'We're home!' said Pinky.

They both realised they had travelled to the future.

50 'We have to do something to save the Earth,' said Chotu.

'I have an idea! Let's make a list of Earth promises to help protect our environment.'

'That's a great idea,' said Pinky. They both sat down and started to write their promises.

8.5 Read and respond

Earth promises

1. We will not use plastic bags.
2. We will not waste water.
3. We will recycle our rubbish.
4. We will not waste food.
5. We will plant more trees.

They ran to their friends and family to talk about their experience and to share their Earth promises!

6. Compare the Earth promises Chotu and Pinky made to the ones you made on page 133. Are any of yours the same as theirs?

7. What emotions did the children experience? What made them feel like this?

8. Would you like to visit the place in the story?

9. **Values:** Being responsible for our environment

   Look back over the unit.
   What new values have you learned during this unit about the environment?

10. Imagine you opened one of the other doors in the story.
    Draw a picture of what you saw.
    Describe it to your partner and compare your pictures.

8 Nature matters

> 8.6 Project challenge

Project A: Make a poster

Be a planet protector! Design a poster about one of these:

- reduce
- reuse
- recycle.

1. Work in pairs or in small groups. Decide which 'R' poster your group is going to create.

2. Look back over the unit and make notes on your 'R' word. Draw and complete a diagram similar to the one below.

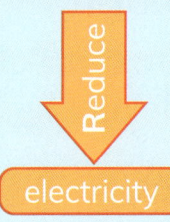

Reduce: electricity
Reuse: clothes
Recycle: card/paper

3. Write a paragraph about the actions we have to take to protect our planet. Stick it on your poster.

4. Design your poster with your group.
    - Find pictures in magazines or on the internet to decorate your poster.
    - Draw pictures too!
    - Stick your paragraph on the poster.
    - Find real objects or materials to stick on your poster.

> To be a planet protector, we have to ride our bikes more. We also have to…

5. Display your posters in the school corridors or in your classroom for other children to read.

8.6 Project challenge

Project B: Design your own recycled monster

1. Work in pairs or small groups. Look back at the story on pages 136–138. Look at the picture of the monster. What type of recycled objects is it made of?

2. Read the sentences and write **true** or **false**.

   a It's made of old wheels. **true** / **false**

   b It's made of computer screens. **true** / **false**

   c It's made of plastic bottles. **true** / **false**

   d It's made of wood. **true** / **false**

   e It's made of cans. **true** / **false**

3. What are these recycled monsters made out of? Tell a partner.

4. Find some of these materials at home or at school to make your recycled monster out of.

5. Draw your design.

6. In groups work on your model monster.
   You'll need glue, scissors, tape and coloured pens.

7. Write a description about your monster. Remember to:

   • give your monster a name   • write about what it's made of.

   a Why did you choose these materials?

   b Does you monster have a special mission?

8. Present your monster to the class.

How well did you communicate with your group on the project?
What might you do differently next time?

8 Nature matters

> 8.7 What do you know now?

What's happening to our Earth and what can we do to make a difference?

1 Which work of art did you like best in lesson 8.1? Compare and explain why to your partner.

2 Make a list of different kinds of pollution on the Earth.

3 What is being affected by these types of pollution?

Our health...

4 Write the names of three things we can:

a reduce   b reuse   c recycle.

5 What do you think is the biggest problem facing our planet?

6 What changes can you make in your everyday habits?

7 What positive things did Chotu and Pinky do after their trip to the future?

Look what I can do!

Write or show examples in your notebook.

I can talk about environmental problems affecting our Earth.

I can understand how our rubbish habits affect the Earth.

I can talk about the impact our habits have on the environment.

I can write a personal recount about a local natural habitat.

I can understand a short story about the future.

9 School's out!

We are going to…

- **talk about** holiday challenges using **would like**
- **research** and **plan** summer camp activities
- **plan** for an adventure trip using **going to**
- **write** an invitation for an end-of-term celebration
- **read** and enjoy a play about going back to school after holidays
- **create** a project with an adventure theme.

Getting started

How can we learn from activities?

a Do you like doing activities like the ones in the pictures? What can you learn?
b What kind of activities do you do in the long school holidays?
c What makes your favourite activities enjoyable?

Watch this!

143

9 School's out!

> 9.1 Do you like a challenge?

We are going to...
- talk about holiday challenges.

1 **Talk** in pairs. What do you think a challenge is? Think of some examples. What could a 'holiday challenge' be? How can a challenge be good for you?

2 **Vocabulary:** Put the verbs and nouns together to make holiday activities. You can use some verbs more than once. Which ones can you see in the photos?

> make   bake   go   explore   design

> a t-shirt   a den   rock climbing   friends   a cake   on a zipwire   a new place

a

b

c

d

3 **Talk** about which activities you have tried. Which ones would you like to try? Why?

9.1 Think about it

🎧 52 **4** **Listen:** What big 'holiday challenge' does the teacher, Ms Sharma, give her students? Which activities does she mention?

🎧 53 **5** Listen to the three girls talking about the holiday challenge. Which activity do they talk about? Do they all want to try it?

🎧 53 **6** Listen again and complete the girls' conversation. Why does Lia want to try rock climbing?

> **Lia:** I'm going to ask my mum if I can go indoor rock climbing. If she says yes, ¹_____ too?
>
> **Mina:** ²_____, I'd love to! When can we go?
>
> **Lia:** I don't know. I need to ask my mum, but I'm sure it will be okay. How about you, Ava? ³_____ too?
>
> **Ava:** Umm, ⁴_____, it's not really my thing. I'd like to try…

7 Look at the phrases 1–4 in Activity 6. Which phrase do we use to invite someone to do something? How can we reply?

> **Language focus – Comparative and superlative adverbs**
>
> We use **comparative** and **superlative** adverbs to compare actions.
> I want to try **harder** and climb **more quickly.**
> We can see who can climb the **fastest**!

8 Complete the sentences with the correct form of the adverb. Use the examples in the Language focus to help you.

  a   Rock climbing starts at 10 am – don't arrive (late) than 9.45 am. (comparative)
  b   Put your equipment on (careful), then it will fit better. (comparative)
  c   Who climbed the (high) in the rock climbing challenge? (superlative)

9 Work on your own first. Make a list of three new challenges to try in the next school holiday. Say why.

10 Talk: In pairs, take turns to invite each other to try the challenges. Say why you want to do these activities.

Would you like to bake a cake?

Yes, I'd love to.

I want to try rock climbing because it makes your arms and legs stronger.

145

9 School's out!

> 9.2 Features of a web page

We are going to...
- research and plan summer camp activities.

Reading tip

Using pictures

Before you read, look at the pictures to help you predict the content and understand the text better.

1 **Vocabulary:** Look at the web pages. Match the words to the icons. What do you use them for?

> web address URLs   refresh   bookmark star   address bar
> minimise   go forward   go back

2 Class 4A is deciding which summer camp they would like to go on. Look at the pictures before you read and talk about the camp activities. Which one would you like to try?

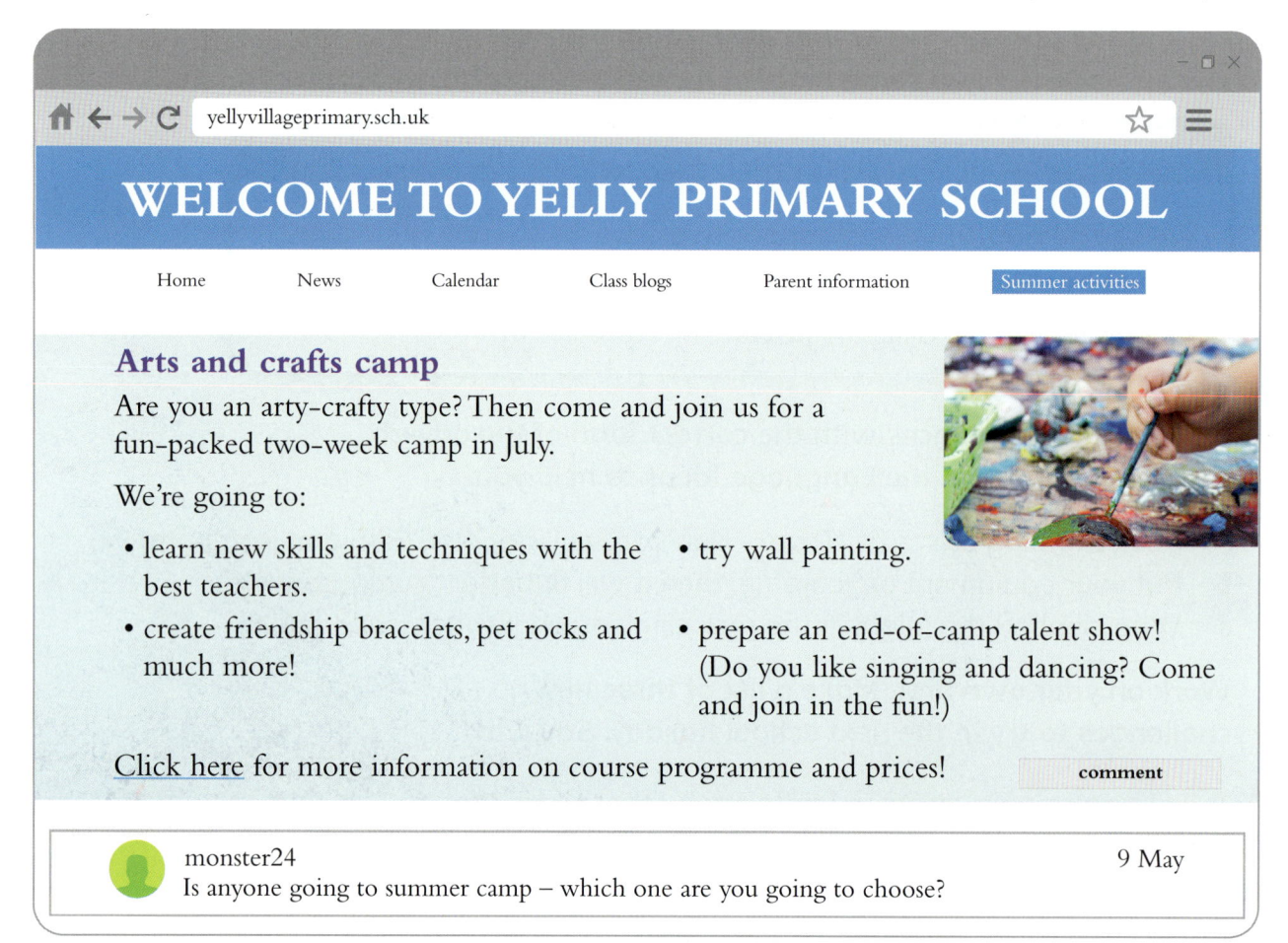

---

yellyvillageprimary.sch.uk

WELCOME TO YELLY PRIMARY SCHOOL

Home   News   Calendar   Class blogs   Parent information   Summer activities

Arts and crafts camp

Are you an arty-crafty type? Then come and join us for a fun-packed two-week camp in July.

We're going to:

- learn new skills and techniques with the best teachers.
- create friendship bracelets, pet rocks and much more!
- try wall painting.
- prepare an end-of-camp talent show! (Do you like singing and dancing? Come and join in the fun!)

Click here for more information on course programme and prices!

comment

monster24   9 May
Is anyone going to summer camp – which one are you going to choose?

9.2 Digital literacy

Adventure camp

Are you an energetic outdoor person? Then join us for our two-week camp in August.

We're going to:

- learn how to survive in the wild – building shelters and making fires.
- discover local flora (wild flowers and trees) and wildlife on our nature trails.
- sing songs and tell scary stories around the campfire!

Click here for more information!

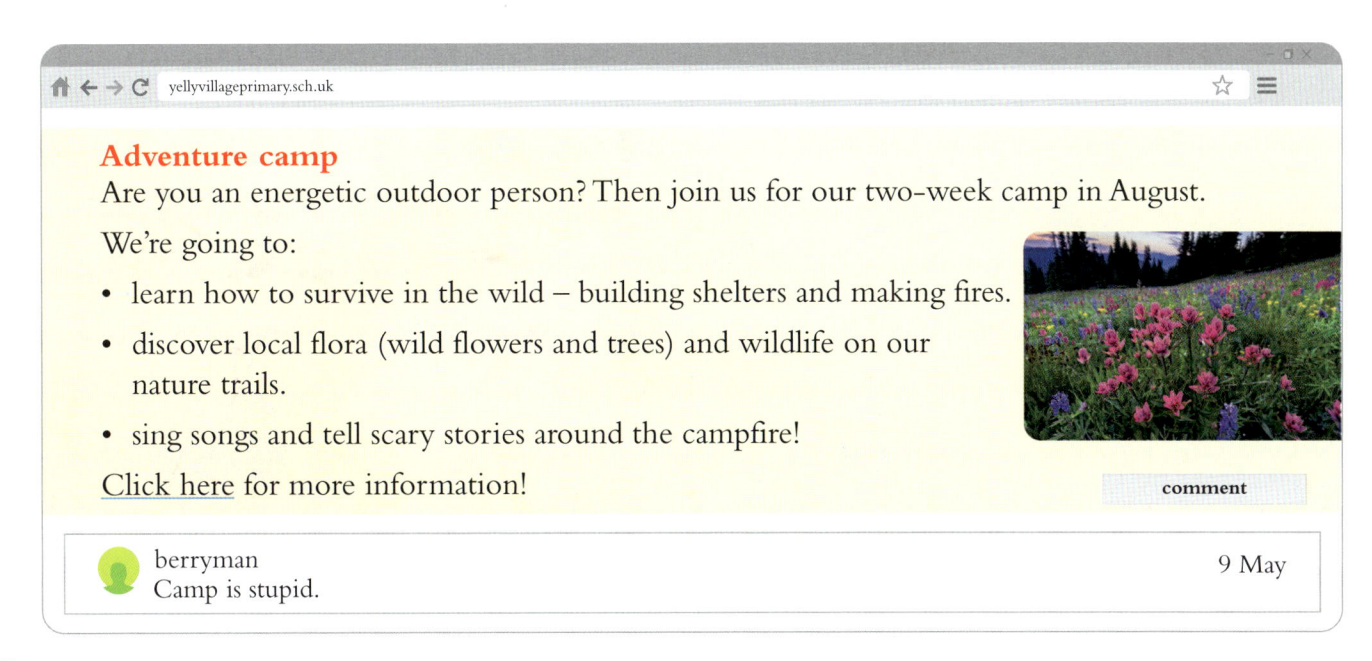

comment

berryman
Camp is stupid.

9 May

3 **Read and listen** to the web page about the summer camps. Answer the questions.

a Which type of camp would you like to go on? Why?
b Which activities have you done before?
c Which activity do you think looks the most interesting?
d How can you tell that this is a school webpage?
e How can you tell which country it's in?

4 Read the 'comments' section again. In pairs, ask and answer the questions.

a Do the children use their own names?
b What identities do the children choose? Why do you think this is a good idea?
c What do you think about the second comment? Is this good online behaviour?

> **Language detective – Going to**
>
> We use **going to** to talk about plans in the future.
>
> **You're going to** learn how to survive in the wild.
>
> **We're going to** sing songs.

5 **Talk:** What other activities are they going to do at the camps described on the website?

6 **In groups, design your own web page with a summer activity advert.**

Step 1: Draw your web page – draw icons and headings to click on.

Step 2: Choose a summer camp to advertise (technology camp, sports camp).

Step 3: Write information about your camp (when, where) and what you can do there.

Step 4: Display your web pages and make comments.

147

9 School's out!

> 9.3 Trip essentials

We are going to…
- pack for an adventure trip.

> We'd need a tent and a sleeping bag for a camping trip.

1 **Vocabulary:** In pairs, talk about what you would need to pack for different kinds of trips. Use the words below.

---

torch   jeans   waterproof jacket   sleeping bag   sweatshirt

shorts   sun cream   tracksuit bottoms   sunglasses   cap   socks

backpack   t-shirt   tent   helmet   insect repellent

---

2 **Talk:** In pairs, use the phrases below to describe the objects in Activity 1. Can your partner guess what you are describing?

- keep you dry
- you sleep in
- protect you
- give light
- you wear
- carry things
- you can fold up

> This keeps you dry.

> Is it a waterproof jacket?

3 Look at the photo. What kind of adventure trip is Kyra doing? What do you think is in her backpack?

4 **Listen:** What six things do Kyra and her friend pack before the trip? How many did you guess correctly from Activity 3?

9.3 Talk about it

5 Match these sentence halves from the girls' conversation. Then listen again and check.

1 How about
2 Why don't we
3 Let's
4 What about

a take shorts too.
b a waterproof jacket and jeans?
c packing a torch?
d take tracksuit bottoms?

Speaking tip

Making suggestions

We can use the phrases in **blue** in Activity 5 to make suggestions and find solutions.

6 **Pronunciation:** Listen and repeat the girls' suggestions. Where does your voice go up and down? Use your hands to follow the sounds!

7 **Write** six things the girls pack and the reasons why. Do you agree with their choices? Would you take anything different? Use these words to help you.

light   hot   dry   wet   warm   cold

Shorts – it might be hot during the day…

8 Which 'special' things do the girls pack? What special thing would you take on a trip like this? Why?

9 **Talk:** In pairs, choose an adventure trip (or choose your own trip).
- Choose seven important things to take in one backpack.
- Choose one 'special' item each.
- Discuss your choices and make suggestions.

10 Find another pair who chose the same trip. Compare your choices for what to take. Which are similar and which are different? Compare your reasons for your decisions.

Why don't we take a…?

9 School's out!

> 9.4 End-of-year celebration

We are going to…
- write an invitation for an end-of-year celebration.

1   **Talk** in pairs. What information do you need to include on an invitation to a party or another event? Tick the information below.

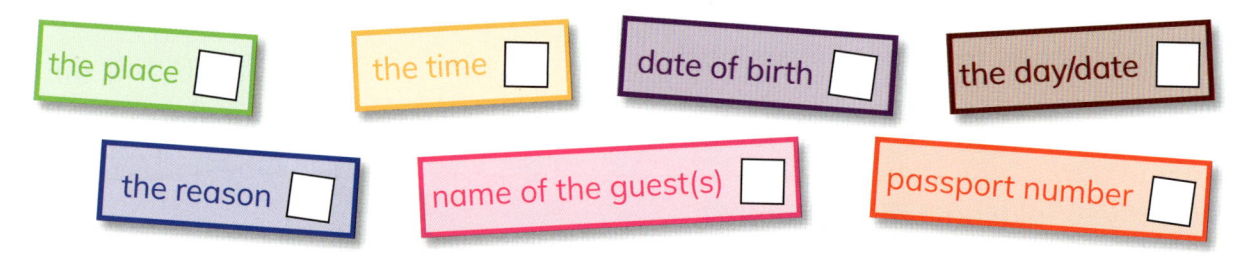

- the place ☐
- the time ☐
- date of birth ☐
- the day/date ☐
- the reason ☐
- name of the guest(s) ☐
- passport number ☐

2   **Read** the invitation below and check your answers to Activity 1.

Dear parents,

[Invitation] We would like to invite you to our end-of-year celebration next Friday at 5pm. We are going to organise different activities in the school grounds to have fun. There are going to be [Future plans] craft activities where you can paint t-shirts and make friendship bracelets. Or you can join in or watch sports activities like running races. When you are hungry you can visit the refreshment tent where you can try our freshly baked cakes or delicious fruit smoothies! Please come along! [Persuasive language] It's going to be a fun afternoon!

Class 4B

9.4 Write about it

3 Copy these circles in your notebook. Write activities from the invitation in each circle. Write three more of your own.

- Craft
- Sport
- Refreshments

4 Read the invitation again then cover the text. Can you remember …
   a a phrase for making an invitation
   b two future plans
   c an example of **persuasive** language (when you want someone to do something).

5 Write an invitation to your end-of-year celebration.

Step 1: Ideas	• In groups, draw. Write **Craft**, **Sports** and **Refreshments** on three separate big pieces of paper. • Write your ideas on the paper. • Stick the pieces of paper around the classroom for other groups to see.
Step 2: Planning your invitation	Read the class ideas. Choose two ideas from each section that you like best.
Step 3: Writing	Write your invitation using the model in Activity 2 to help you.
Step 4: Read, compare and check.	• Swap with a partner. • Check for spelling and grammar mistakes! • Compliment each other:

Writing tip

Capital letters

Use capital letters for days of the week: **Friday**

I like this activity!

6 Present, display or publish your work.

9 School's out!

9.5 Back to school!

We are going to...

- read a play about going back to school after holidays.

1 **Talk** in pairs, talk about how you feel about going back to school after long holidays. What are the good and bad things about going back to school?

2 In pairs, look at the picture and the title of the play. How do you think the children are feeling? Why?

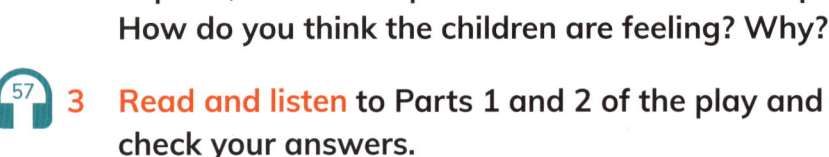

3 **Read and listen** to Parts 1 and 2 of the play and check your answers.

Back to School!

Part 1

[Ben, Tom and Daisy are sitting together looking unhappy.]

Ben: I really don't want to start school again tomorrow.

5 **Daisy: Me neither.**

Ben: The holidays have been great. I don't want them to end!

Tom: Me neither.

Ben: I keep thinking about tomorrow
10 and going back to school. My stomach feels funny and I feel a bit sick!

Daisy: Me too!

Ben: I don't want to start a new class with that new teacher!

15 **Tom:** Me neither!

Ben: I liked our old class. I want to go back there!

Daisy: Me too!

Ben: I'm going to tell my mum and dad
20 that I'm not going to school tomorrow!

Tom: Me too!

Ben: What? You're going to tell *my* mum and dad that *you're* not going to school tomorrow?

25 **Tom:** Nooo...! It's just that I feel the same and I've never told anyone before...I always feel like this the day before going back to school after the holidays...

30 **Ben: Me too...**

Daisy: Me too...

9.5 Read and respond

Part 2

[The three children nod glumly. Ben's older sister, Sara, approaches.]

Sara: Hey, how's it going? Oh, dear! What's the matter?

Ben: Nothing! Nothing at all!

Tom: Nooo…nothing! We're great, aren't we?

Sara: No, you're not! I can tell…I know what it is…you're feeling nervous because you've got to go back to school tomorrow, aren't you?

Daisy: No!

Tom: Well, actually, yeah…you're right.

Sara: I thought so. Look, it's okay. Everyone feels like that the night before. I'm feeling a bit like that too…

Ben: Really? But you're fourteen!

Sara: I know, but I still get that feeling. Everyone does! Look, there will be loads of kids, everywhere, who are feeling exactly the same way today.

Daisy: Do you really think so?

Sara: Sure! Kids everywhere get this feeling, whatever their age. It's just that no one admits it! And it's not just kids…

Ben: You mean…?

Sara: Yes! Even adults get it too. Dad told me once that even he gets a bit nervous before he goes back to work after a holiday. He said that he thinks about the great big pile of work waiting for him on his desk…hundreds of emails in his inbox…and he's 42!

Ben: Well, I suppose it's normal to feel like this if even adults get it …

Tom: And big sisters…

Sara: Of course it is! Think of all the good things too…there are good things about going back to school, you know. Try to think of some!

Daisy: Well, it'll be really good to see all our friends again. It's been ages since we've seen most of them.

Tom: And the football season starts when we go back!

4 Read and listen to Part 1 again and answer the questions.

a How do the children feel? What is the main reason?
b What other reasons does Ben give for the way he feels?
c What does he plan to do? Do you think he's serious?

153

9 School's out!

5 Read and listen to Part 2 again and answer the questions.

a Does Ben's older sister, Sara, feel the same way?
b Sara says that no one knows that everyone has the same feeling. Why is this?
c What does Sara say to make the children feel better about their problem?
d What examples does she give to support what she says?
e What is her advice in the end?

6 Word study: Find the responses in blue in the play that go with these sentences.

a I really don't want to start school again tomorrow. *Me neither.*
b The holidays have been great. I don't want them to end!
c My stomach feels funny and I feel a bit sick!
d I liked our old class. I want to go back there!
e I always feel like this…
f I'm feeling a bit like that too…

7 Talk: Think about your own feelings. Use the words in blue from the play to respond to these statements.

a I can't wait to go back to school tomorrow!
Really?
b I wish the holidays were longer.
c I'd like to have more homework.
d I think we have too much homework.
e I don't feel ready to go back to school tomorrow.
f I don't want the holidays to end.

Language focus – Question tags

We add **question tags** to make sentences into questions.

We use them to check information or invite someone to agree with us.

We're great, **aren't we**?
You're feeling nervous… **aren't you**?

9.5 Read and respond

8 Look at the examples in the Language focus. Can you correct the question tags?

a You love going back to school, **do / don't** you?
b He's not happy about it, **is / isn't** he?

9 Listen and repeat. Why do you think exclamation marks are used in writing?

a …and he's 42!
b I feel a bit sick!
c Nothing! Nothing at all!
d Of course it is!

10 Listen to the sentences again and answer the questions.

a Which speaker is upset?
b Which speaker is trying to hide something?
c Which speaker wants to emphasise that something is correct?
d Which speaker wants to emphasise something surprising or funny?

11 In groups of four, act out the play.

- Choose a role each and practise reading the play first. Remember to put expression in your voices.
- Now act out the play together. If you all feel confident, act it out in front of your class!

12 Values: Being sympathetic

In the play, Sara listened to the children's problems and tried to help.
In pairs, create a role play using one of these problems (or think of one of your own).

- You're on a school trip to an adventure park. One of the activities is a zipwire and you're feeling very nervous.
- You couldn't finish your holiday homework and are afraid to tell the teacher.

Student A: Explain the problem to your friend.

Student B: Respond to your friend and try to help

I feel really nervous about going on the zipwire!

Me too. But you'll be fine. It's very safe and…

9 School's out!

9.6 Project challenge

Project A: A nature trail map

1 Work in pairs. What types of environments can you see?
   Make a list of types of wildlife you might see in each one in your country.

2 Class 4B has been on a nature trail. Look at the map. What type of environment is it? Would you find this wildlife in your country?

3 Organise a nature trail near your school.

Step 1	• Take a notepad and pen on your trip. • Look for insects, trees, animals, or any wildlife around. • Write what you see. Where did you see it? What was it doing?
Step 2	Draw and complete your nature trail map. • Draw a map of your route with points of interest. • Draw and label a simple picture of each animal you saw. Mark where you saw it on your map. • Find information about its characteristics, its habitat and its diet. • Write a short description. Stick it next to your drawing.

9.6 Project challenge

Project B: Create a short play

1. Match each fear to photos a–e below.
   - Afraid of heights
   - Afraid of thunderstorms
   - Afraid of the water
   - Afraid of spiders
   - Afraid of the dark

2. Imagine you and your classmates are going on an adventure trip. Some of your friends are nervous. In groups, choose one of the following issues to write a short play about.

3. Choose two characters for your play and think of a title.

4. Write a short dialogue between the characters. One character explains their problem and the other should be sympathetic to the other character's problems and try to help.

   Remember to:

   - use **sympathetic language**

   - use **exclamation marks (!)** to emphasise strong points and emotions

   - add **notes to the script** to let the reader know what the characters are doing. [Gema and Ivan are sitting together on the coach. Gema is looking upset]

   > You'll be fine. Everything will be OK.

   > I feel so nervous about...!

5. Practise and perform your play in groups. If you feel confident, perform it in front of the class.

What was the most important thing you learned when working on your project?

9 School's out!

> 9.7 What do you know now?

How can we learn from activities?

1. Name five activities from lesson 9.1 (verb + noun phrase). Which ones have you tried?

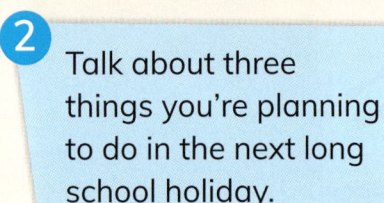

2. Talk about three things you're planning to do in the next long school holiday.

3. You and a friend are going camping. Suggest four things to take and give a reason why.

4. Invite two friends to do some activities with you next weekend. Say what you are going to do, when and where.

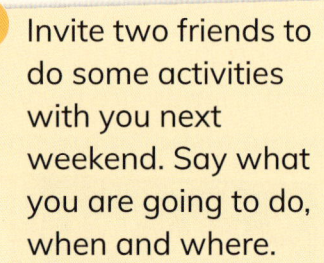

5. In the play Back to school, what did Sara say to make the children feel better about going back to school after the holidays?

Let's take a ___ to keep us dry when it rains.

Look what I can do!

Write or show examples in your notebook.

I can give examples of challenging activities.

I can research information and plan summer camp activities.

I can use 'going to' to talk about plans.

I can make suggestions about packing for an adventure trip.

I can write an invitation for an end-of-term celebration.

I can understand a short play.

I can read lines from the play using expression in my voice.

Check your progress 3

1 Find three words for each category below in the word puzzle.

> drought   blizzard   tornado   global warming   pollution   eco-friendly   desert
> coast   coral reef   zipwire   rock climbing   wall painting

Extreme weather	Geographical features	Environment	Holiday activities

2 Match the definitions to the words in the wordpool above.

   a   a place where marine life lives
   b   a type of product that respects our natural environment
   c   a snowstorm
   d   something that is dangerous for our health and the Earth
   e   a place that is a very dry area with little water
   f   an activity that is creative and fun

3 In pairs, choose and write down six words from Units 7, 8 and 9.

   1 bake a cake
   2
   3
   4
   5
   6

   This is something that you do in the kitchen.

4 Now join with another pair. Take turns to define your words. Can you guess each other's words?

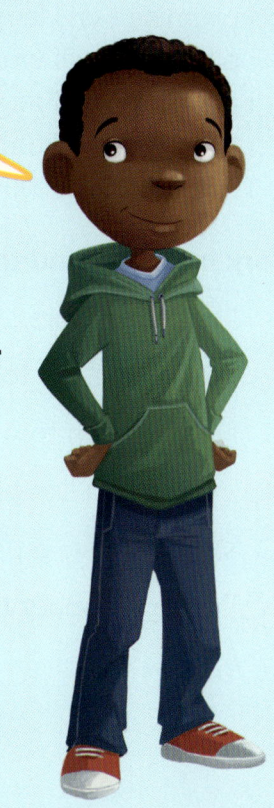

Check your progress 3

5 Follow the instructions.

a Set yourself a holiday challenge. Write down three new activities you are going to do this summer.
I'm going to …

b Find someone else in the class who has the same or similar challenges to you.
Are you going to…?

c Stand with your partner. Tell the class your plans.

6 In pairs, describe the photos. Which activity or trip would you like to try? Talk about what you would need to pack for the trips.

We're going to…

a   b   c   d

7 Read these sentences and write **true** or **false**.

a	I promise I will reuse plastic bags.	true / false
b	I promise I will leave the light on in my room.	true / false
c	I promise I will walk more to school.	true / false
d	I promise I will recycle as much packaging as possible.	true / false
e	I promise I will throw rubbish on the ground.	true / false
f	I promise I will leave the water running when I brush my teeth.	true / false

8 Work in pairs. Find the error or missing word in each sentence.

a I'm do a nature study this afternoon.

b I promise I will to recycle more.

c I never been to Australia.

d Would you like go sightseeing?

e We are have a picnic tomorrow.

f I've learn about the lungfish in class.